Programming Microcontrollers with Python

Experience the Power of Embedded Python

Armstrong Subero

Apress®

Programming Microcontrollers with Python: Experience the Power of Embedded Python

Armstrong Subero
Basse Terre, Moruga, Trinidad and Tobago

ISBN-13 (pbk): 978-1-4842-7057-8   ISBN-13 (electronic): 978-1-4842-7058-5
https://doi.org/10.1007/978-1-4842-7058-5

Managing Director, Apress Media LLC: Welmoed Spahr
Acquisitions Editor: Susan McDermott
Development Editor: James Markham
Coordinating Editor: Jessica Vakili

Distributed to the book trade worldwide by Springer Science+Business Media New York, 1 NY Plaza, New York, NY 10004. Phone 1-800-SPRINGER, fax (201) 348-4505, e-mail orders-ny@springer-sbm.com, or visit www.springeronline.com. Apress Media, LLC is a California LLC and the sole member (owner) is Springer Science + Business Media Finance Inc (SSBM Finance Inc). SSBM Finance Inc is a **Delaware** corporation.

For information on translations, please e-mail booktranslations@springernature.com; for reprint, paperback, or audio rights, please e-mail bookpermissions@springernature.com.

Apress titles may be purchased in bulk for academic, corporate, or promotional use. eBook versions and licenses are also available for most titles. For more information, reference our Print and eBook Bulk Sales web page at http://www.apress.com/bulk-sales.

Any source code or other supplementary material referenced by the author in this book is available to readers on GitHub via the book's product page, located at www.apress.com/978-1-4842-7057-8. For more detailed information, please visit http://www.apress.com/source-code.

Printed on acid-free paper

To all those who tinker to keep the world running

Table of Contents

About the Author

Armstrong Subero started learning electronics at the age of 8. One of
the happiest memories in his childhood was when he finally figured out
how to make a light bulb. It took off from there as he taught himself more
advanced topics in electronics, before delving into computer architecture,
and eventually discovering the joys of microcontrollers and FPGAs.

He currently works for the Ministry of National Security in his country;
writes software; designs circuits, courses, and robots; writes books; and
blogs about technology on www.trinirobotics.com in his free time.
He is also a contributing author to Free Code Camp and has degrees in
Computer Science and Liberal Arts and Sciences from Thomas Edison
State University. He is the author of *Programming PIC Microcontrollers
with XC8* and *Codeless Data Structures and Algorithms* both published by
Apress Media LLC.

About the Technical Reviewer

Sai Yamanoor is an embedded systems engineer working for an industrial gases company in Buffalo, NY. His interests, deeply rooted in DIY and open source hardware, include developing gadgets that aid behavior modification. He has published two books with his brother, and in his spare time, he likes to contribute to build things that improve quality of life. You can find his project portfolio at http://saiyamanoor.com.

Acknowledgments

I want to thank my family.

I want to thank *everyone* who ever said anything positive to me or taught me something. I heard it all, and it meant something.

I want to thank God most of all, because without God I wouldn't be able to do any of this.

## CHAPTER 1

Getting Ready

You have decided to learn about microcontrollers using Python. While it would be nice to jump straight into developing cool stuff, there are a few steps you must take to get ready first. If you have experience with software development, you may be accustomed to just opening an editor and typing code right away. However, microcontroller development is a little more involved than that. After all, you will be writing programs for a separate computer, so there is a lot more to set up. A microcontroller development environment consists of not only software but an entire hardware ecosystem that must be understood to unlock all the magic these devices have to offer.

In this chapter, we will look at setting up an environment for development. By the end of the chapter, you will be ready to select a microcontroller board, and you'll have the software tools and hardware devices needed to begin your development with CircuitPython. Let's get started!

Introduction to Microcontrollers

In our modern world, computers are ubiquitous. They have become smaller, easier to use, and more integrated into our daily lives. A few years ago, to connect to the Internet and check your email, you would have had to sit down at a large desktop device. Today, you can do the same thing with a computer that fits in the palm of your hand and places all the information in the world at your fingertips.

© Armstrong Subero 2021
A. Subero, *Programming Microcontrollers with Python*,
https://doi.org/10.1007/978-1-4842-7058-5_1

The advancements in technology that brought us smartphones and tablets have given billions of people access to computers. However, these handheld devices aren't the only computers that exist. What if I told you that the billions of smartphones in use pale when compared to another kind of computing device that silently surrounds us? In fact, there are probably a half dozen or more of these devices in the room with you right now. These miniature computers are called *microcontrollers*, or *MCUs*, and they can be found all around us.

Microcontrollers are small, intelligent, programmable computers that we use to perform tasks that are repetitive or that require some level of intelligent control without the need for human interaction. Microcontroller devices have a fraction of the computing power of a device like your smartphone or tablet, but they have many, many uses. Any device around you that reacts to a button press, displays information, or makes sounds when something is wrong is most likely controlled by a microcontroller. From calculators to TVs to microwaves and dishwashers, almost every household device you can think of contains a microcontroller.

If you are familiar with computers, you are sure to have heard of a central processing unit (CPU) or a microprocessor: the brain behind your computer. A microprocessor lets a computer perform many functions. One day you might use your computer to type a document, the next to stream your favorite movie, and so on. The microprocessor has a lot of supporting circuitry, including memory and input and output chips, that allows it to carry out all these tasks. These are usually part of the motherboard that houses the microprocessor.

A microcontroller takes all the supporting chips that are required to make a microprocessor work and places them on a single chip. This is why a microcontroller is called a *single-chip computer*. A microcontroller still operates like the microprocessor, but it is designed to only do a single task and to do it as efficiently as possible. For this reason, a microcontroller chip contains the minimum amount of processing power required to do its task.

Firmware, Memory, and Clock Speed

Like general-purpose computers, microcontrollers work by running programs. Because microcontrollers perform limited functions, the programs written for them are not expected to change frequently. For that reason, programs written for microcontrollers are called *firmware*. This firmware is usually stored as a binary file (with a .bin file extension) or a hex file which is a text-represented binary file (having a .hex file extension); this file contains the memory content that is written on flash, and thus it is ready to be run on the microcontroller. A special device called a programmer loads this binary file into the microcontroller's memory.

The memory consists of two parts: the main memory (sometimes called program memory) and the random-access memory (RAM, sometimes called data memory). The main memory is nonvolatile, whereas RAM is volatile. This means that when the microcontroller is not powered, the information contained in RAM will disappear, whereas the information in the main memory will be retained. For this reason, the main memory is also called read-only memory (ROM). Its contents are designed to be mainly read, whereas RAM is designed to have its contents changed by the user during runtime.

In a general-purpose computer system, usually a program is loaded into RAM before it is executed. Microcontroller systems are a bit different. In a microcontroller, the firmware is executed directly from ROM, and RAM is used to do things such as to store temporary information that aids in running the firmware (these are usually runtime variables and can contain a stack or a heap, special memory structures).

Some microcontroller devices can have their ROM contents programmed into them from the factory and cannot be changed by the end user once they are put into a device. These are called one-time programmable (OTP) devices, and they are cheaper and easier to manufacture. Usually though, the ROM is made of flash memory, meaning that it can be programmed and changed after manufacturing.

3

Flash memory lets you program a device thousands of times, making it useful for learning and product prototyping. If errors show up in your firmware program, flash also allows you to fix errors by means of an update, a process called patching. Updates usually take the form of over-the-air (OTA) updates, which change the contents of the ROM via a wireless connection. OTA updates are common for Internet of Things (IoT) devices. Alternately, you can connect the device to a computer with a cable to update the firmware.

A microcontroller executes the instructions in its firmware program according to the speed of a clock that runs the device. The speed is measured in hertz, or cycles per second. The faster the *clock speed*, the faster the device will execute instructions. Microcontroller clock speeds typically range from about 1 MHz (though for extremely low-cost, low-power applications, the clock speed can run as low as 32.768 kHz to about and for fast systems up to 1 GHz.)

8-Bit vs. 32-Bit

The devices we will use in this book are quite powerful. They consist of a 32-bit microprocessor core which means that the number of bits of data that can be processed by the microcontroller is comprised of 32 registers (a register is a small storage location for data within the microcontroller; we'll talk about this more in the next chapter). For a long time, however, 8-bit devices ruled the microcontroller market.

Historically, 32-bit devices were expensive and hard to program. Due to advances in technology, the cost of 32-bit devices has been declining to the point of where they can rival 8-bit devices for all but extremely cost-sensitive applications. Meanwhile, thanks to the myriad of tools now available to use with them, 32-bit devices have become amazingly easy to program and control. While 8-bit microcontrollers are still alive and relevant, a lot of their market share is being replaced by 32-bit devices.

For beginners, 32-bit devices are an especially useful learning tool because they contain more memory and have greater memory addressing capabilities. This allows for a higher level of abstraction, meaning it is typically easier to program a 32-bit device without a thorough understanding of its inner workings. By contrast, since 8-bit devices have less processing power and memory, you need to have a deeper understanding of the internals of the device to better manage memory resources and write effective programs.

Microcontroller Programming Languages

In this section, we will look at some of the languages available for programming microcontrollers. While there are several options to choose from, microcontrollers have been mostly resistant to the overcrowded zoo of programming languages that make up the modern software development landscape. Historically, the microcontroller world has been dominated by the C programming language. This is because microcontrollers have traditionally only had a few bytes of memory and run at a few tens of megahertz of clock speed, and C is particularly well suited to working on memory-constrained systems. Nowadays, though, you can find microcontroller devices that have multiple cores that run up a gigahertz and possess several megabytes of memory, opening up space for other languages to be used.

Assembly Language

At one point in time, microcontrollers were programmed exclusively in assembly language. Today, assembly language is reserved for devices with limited memory and for situations where the programmer needs to squeeze every drop of performance out of the microcontroller. Assembly language is useful in these situations because a lot of assembly instructions translate directly into machine instructions on the microcontroller. This means that there is less overhead in the execution of the instructions, making code segments written in assembly language faster. While assembly language is fast, it takes a lot of instructions to perform a simple task on the device. Another limiting factor of assembly language is that for each device you are programming, you must learn the assembly language for that device. Given these limitations, the language has declined in popularity for all but niche situations.

C

C has long been the language of choice in the embedded world. It was made to run on memory-constrained devices such as microcontrollers. C gives us the ability to control the underlying hardware efficiently – one C instruction translates into several assembly language instructions – and it can match the speed of assembly language for most applications. Since C has been used for so long, a lot of the code that is written has been battle tested and proven to work for the applications they are intended. C users have access to a large code base with helpful information and code snippets. However, the language requires a good understanding of the hardware and is difficult for beginners to break into.

C++

As time progressed and embedded devices became more powerful, some microcontroller manufacturers and software vendors began adding C++ support to their devices. C++ is slowly gaining traction in the professional embedded space. In the hobbyist realm, however, C++ finds widespread use on the Arduino platform. C++ is a large and difficult language to learn, however. Many of the features that make C++ more effective to use than C in general-purpose computing applications, sometimes cannot be implemented on the resource-constrained microcontroller devices. This is because while C++ can match the performance of C for most applications, C++ tends to use more memory, a precious resource that is usually not bountiful on microcontroller devices. For that reason, C++ is reserved for the higher-end devices.

BASIC

In the early 2000s, if a beginner was getting started with microcontrollers and did not fancy assembly, BASIC was the programming language to use. BASIC stands for Beginners' All-Purpose Symbolic Instruction Code and is an easy programming language to use. There would usually be a BASIC interpreter on the microcontroller chip to run the instructions.

BASIC eventually fell in popularity because the boards that ran it cost a lot of money relative to what they were capable of. Additionally, running the BASIC interpreter slowed the chips down and took up too many resources on the already constrained 8-bit devices. Also, the tools and software for the most popular BASIC devices were all closed source, so people could not make their own BASIC devices. When open source alternatives like the Arduino came around, devices like the BASIC Stamp thus fell out of favor.

Rust

The Rust programming language is new compared to C (which is almost half a century old) and is designed to upset the C and C++ hold on systems programming, including embedded programming. As microcontrollers become more powerful and factors like concurrency (the ability to carry out multiple processes at once) start to matter, Rust's advantages over C begin to show. Rust is better suited to concurrency because it can handle a data race, which is when two devices try to access the same location in memory at the same time.

While Rust could replace C, there is no reason for the industry to adopt it anytime soon. Embedded software is called firmware for a reason: it doesn't change all that often, and much of the code that has already been written has no reason to change to a new language. C works and has a lot of established toolchains and devices, and there are many skilled developers comfortable with the language. However, there are already tools available that allow Rust to be used on microcontrollers, and as time progresses, Rust may gain some share in the embedded market.

Python

Python is a relative newcomer to the embedded space, and it could become a major player in the field. Python is a lot simpler than C to learn and is one of the most popular programming languages today. While BASIC was also easier than C for beginners, Python has several advantages over BASIC that make it better suited for use as an embedded language. Notably, while the popular BASIC microcontrollers were closed source, Python is open source, allowing you to run Python on your custom device if you desire. Python files can also be compiled to make them smaller, allowing you to create tight, memory-efficient programs.

Many people say that interpreted languages like Python are not suited to the limitations of microcontrollers. This may have once been true, but with today's more powerful devices, it is entirely possible for microcontrollers to run interpreted languages without hiccups like the speed limitations experienced by older BASIC devices. For extremely time-efficient computing, also called real-time computing, interpreted languages are still not suitable. However, Python should have no problem meeting the speed requirements of the majority of microcontroller projects.

While Python is not as fast or efficient as C when running on microcontrollers, its ease of use makes it worthwhile, especially if you are now getting started with microcontrollers. Additionally, you can extend Python code with C, which means you can leverage existing C code bases that have been battle tested and refined over the decades.

The Python interpreter as it exists on general-purpose computers cannot be directly implemented on a microcontroller with the same available features. This is because the standard Python interpreter is a large program that relies on features that would be given by the operating system, particularly memory and hardware interfacing features, a luxury nonexistent on microcontroller devices. Two modified forms of the language interpreter, MicroPython and CircuitPython, bridge the gap between the standard Python interpreter and the embedded space. Of the two, MicroPython is targeted more toward professional developers and precedes CircuitPython. CircuitPython, developed by Adafruit, is simpler to use, making it an excellent learning tool for beginners as well as a platform for professionals. The major feature of CircuitPython that makes it user-friendly is that you do not need to compile a program before it can run on the microcontroller. As soon as you save a program, it is run and executed.

CircuitPython promises to be available for more resource-constrained devices and is expected to remain well supported into the foreseeable future. For these reasons, we will use it throughout this book.

Selecting a Development Board

To work on the projects in this book, you will need a development board with a microcontroller that can run CircuitPython. A development board contains a microcontroller as well as the connections required to power the board and get it up and running. A development board allows you to use, program, and prototype with the microcontroller without worrying about the hardware setup.

At the time of writing, CircuitPython supports over 140 boards, and the list keeps growing. You can view the list here on the CircuitPython website: `https://circuitpython.org/downloads`. Any one of these compatible boards will work with this book. You can also choose to create your own custom device that supports CircuitPython, a process I will discuss at the end of this chapter. For beginners, however, using a premade, CircuitPython-compatible board will always be a better choice. It will ensure that the hardware is working and allow you to get started more quickly with writing software for your device.

In this section, we will look at some preconfigured devices that can run CircuitPython. Though many companies supply microcontroller boards that are capable of running CircuitPython, Adafruit devices have the best support since they originated the language and have an entire ecosystem built around CircuitPython with their development environment. We'll look at some of the boards that they have available, along with some popular boards from other manufacturers that can be used with CircuitPython. This list is not exhaustive, but the boards presented here will be compatible with the examples discussed in this book.

Adafruit Metro M0 Express

The first board we will look at is the Adafruit Metro M0 Express, pictured in Figure 1-1. This board is an ideal choice to be used with the examples in this book, as it is powered by a SAMD21G18A microcontroller. This board also has the Arduino form factor; this means that it can be used with existing Arduino shields. Thus, the powerful Arduino ecosystem can be used to easily prototype with Arduino shields in Python. The SAMD21G18A represents the "ideal minimum" that is required to run

CircuitPython. Its features allow it to run the interpreter without any hiccups. The SAMD21G18A has a 48 MHz clock, 256KB of flash memory, and 32KB of RAM. (For comparison, boards powered by the ATmega328 microcontroller, like the Arduino Uno, offered 8 times less flash and 16 times less RAM.) The Metro M0 Express also has 2MB of flash storage that can be used to store programs and other files. You may be able to run the CircuitPython interpreter with less memory or less processing power than the SAMD21G18A offers, but the experience may not be seamless.

The SAMD21G18A microcontroller was one of the first devices to support CircuitPython, and boards built around this device are usually among the first to receive the newest versions of the interpreter. In particular, the Metro M0 Express was the first Adafruit Metro board designed to use CircuitPython. It is considered the standard board for running CircuitPython, and it will be able to run the programs in this book decently.

Figure 1-1. *Adafruit Metro M0 Express [Credit: Adafruit, adafruit.com]*

Adafruit Feather M0 Express

If you want a more minimalist approach to development, you can grab the Feather M0 Express from Adafruit, shown in Figure 1-2. Because it is also built around the SAMD21G18A processor, this board has all the capabilities of the Metro M0 Express: the same 48 MHz clock, 256KB of flash, and 32KB of RAM. It also has the same onboard 2MB of flash storage. However, it is more compact than the Metro, and it has 5 fewer I/O pins – 20 rather than 25.

A cool feature of this board that the Metro M0 Express lacks is the little prototyping area in the front. When you have become acquainted with the Metro M0 Express and you want a board to embed into your own projects, then you can use this smaller, cheaper board. There is also the QT Py board from Adafruit which is even more compact than the M0 Express should you need an even smaller board for your projects.

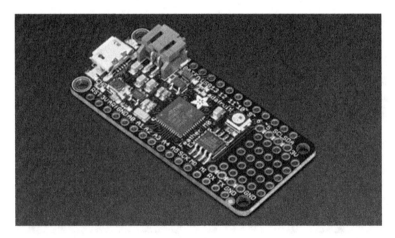

Figure 1-2. *Adafruit Feather M0 Express [Credit: Adafruit, adafruit.com]*

Adafruit Metro M4 Express

If you need a little more oomph than the Metro M0 Express offers, then you can grab the Metro M4 Express, shown in Figure 1-3. The board is powered by the SAMD51J19 microcontroller, which offers better performance than the SAMD21G18A-based devices discussed earlier. At 120 MHz, it runs at more than double the clock speed of the SAMD21G18A-based boards, and it features 512KB of flash memory, 192KB of RAM, and an additional 2MB of onboard flash storage.

These enhanced features provide better support for digital signal processing (DSP) and floating-point processing applications. If you want to use your board for applications like audio processing, or if you're looking for better security capability or general performance improvement, then this is a good board to use. However, the heightened performance comes with a trade-off. The Metro M4 Express's processor will consume more power than the boards discussed earlier. Depending on your application, this may not be much of a factor, though, as the board is still power efficient.

Figure 1-3. *Adafruit M4 Metro Express [Credit: Adafruit, adafruit.com]*

13

Adafruit Grand Central M4 Express

The next board we can use to work along with this book is the Adafruit Grand Central M4 Express, pictured in Figure 1-4. This board is quite powerful compared to the Metro M0, as it features an ATSAMD51P20 microcontroller. It runs 2.5 times faster, and the RAM size of this board is 8 times that of the Metro M0. In fact, the Grand Central has the same amount of RAM as the entire flash memory of the Metro M0 (let that sink in a bit). The Grand Central also has 1MB of flash memory, 8MB of onboard flash storage via a QSPI chip, and a built-in SD card socket. The board also has almost three times the I/O present on the Metro M0. When you have a large application and run out of space (either memory or I/O) on a more basic board, this board is a good migration path.

The Grand Central can definitely be used to run all the examples in this book, and when you're ready to move on to your own, more sophisticated CircuitPython projects, boards like this one that use an ATSAMD51 microcontroller are an ideal choice. Applications such as machine learning and video game programming can be done with this board due to its ample resources.

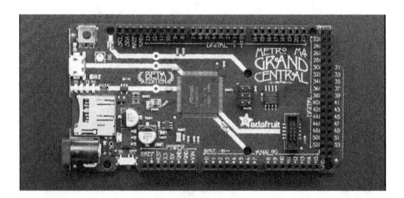

Figure 1-4. *Adafruit Grand Central M4 Express [Credit: Adafruit, adafruit.com]*

The Arduino Zero

The Arduino Uno was undoubtedly one of the most popular microcontroller boards to have ever existed, and it is still widely used today. It showed us that 8-bit microcontrollers are highly capable. However, the world is changing, and 32-bit microcontrollers have taken over a lot of market segments that were once controlled by 8-bit devices. The Arduino Uno platform has many limitations, and for that reason the Arduino Zero was created to bring the world of 32-bit development into the Arduino universe. The Arduino Zero in Figure 1-5 was a step toward making 32-bit embedded computing accessible to users of the Arduino platform.

The Arduino Zero is powered by the SAMD21G18A microcontroller, the same one used in the Metro M0 and Feather M0 boards. While it lacks the onboard flash storage present on the Adafruit Metro boards, the Arduino can still run decent sized programs and will work with all the examples provided in this book. Unlike the other boards discussed earlier, which while open source (yes, all the hardware schematics as well as source code is available) are specific to one vendor, the Arduino Zero has many clones of the board that you will be able to run CircuitPython on. These clones are often cheaper than the official boards from the manufacturer.

Figure 1-5. *The Arduino Zero [Credit: Adafruit, adafruit.com]*

The STM32F746ZG Nucleo

STM32-based boards can also run the examples discussed in this book. For instance, the STM32F746ZG Nucleo was tested with all the examples in this book and will run fine. This board, shown in Figure 1-6, is an absolute monster. It features the STM32F746ZG microcontroller, whose processor offers greater performance than any of the boards discussed earlier. The board runs at a staggering 216 MHz and has 320KB of RAM and 1MB of flash memory.

The STM32F746ZG is targeted more toward people with previous microcontroller experience. While it does run well with CircuitPython, it's not as out-of-the-box friendly as the other boards presented in this lineup. Still, the speed and performance of the board makes it worth using to perform computationally intensive tasks with CircuitPython such as decoding MP3 files or using Ethernet or when you need a lot of I/O.

If you want even more juice, you can look at getting the STM32H743 Nucleo, which has a microcontroller that runs up to 400 MHz. With 1MB of RAM and 2MB of flash, it works comfortably with CircuitPython. This board is also not as beginner-friendly as some of the others, and it comes with some gotchas. For example, some of the exotic peripherals on the microcontroller may not be available for use in CircuitPython without support for yourself. These include peripherals like the HDMI, DFSDM, and Op Amps. Also, since the board runs at 400 MHz, it draws a lot of power, so it's not ideal for battery-powered applications. New microcontroller users may be better off starting with one of the Metro boards before moving to this one.

Figure 1-6. *The STM32F746ZG Nucleo*

Device Comparison

Table 1-1 compares the features of the boards that can be used to follow along with this book. It can be a daunting task to select the right microcontroller to use. The best overall microcontroller in my opinion is the Adafruit Grand Central M4 as it is powerful and well supported by CircuitPython. However, any of the boards discussed earlier will work for our purposes.

17

Table 1-1. *Device Comparison*

Device	Clock Speed	RAM	FLASH	ONBOARD SPI FLASH MEMORY
Metro M0	48 MHz	32KB	256KB	2MB
Feather M0	48 MHz	32KB	256KB	2MB
Metro M4	120 MHz	192KB	512KB	2MB
Grand Central M4	120 MHz	265KB	1MB	8MB
Arduino Zero	48 MHz	32KB	256KB	NONE
STM32F746ZG Nucleo	216 MHz	320KB	1MB	NONE

The Component List

The microcontroller is at the heart of our circuits. However, the projects in this book will also require supporting components and devices. Table 1-2 lists all the devices and components you will need to follow along with this book. Don't worry: Each component will be discussed in detail as it arises. For your convenience, the table provides two product numbers for each item, one from Amazon and one from another vendor. You're welcome to shop around for other options that fit the item descriptions, however.

Table 1-2. *Component List*

Item	Quantity	Vendor	Product Number
Assorted Resistor Kit	1	Jameco	2217511
		Amazon ASIN	B07L851T3V
10K Breadboard Trim Potentiometer	2	Adafruit	356
		Amazon ASIN	B07S69443J
Capacitors 220 µF Electrolytic	1	Adafruit	2192
		Amazon ASIN	B07SBW1Y17
Capacitors 0.1 µF Ceramic	1	Adafruit	753
		Amazon ASIN	B07RB4W4MR
5mm Red LEDs	1	Adafruit	299
		Amazon ASIN	B077X95F7C
Tactile Switch Pushbuttons	1	Adafruit	1119
		Amazon ASIN	B01GN79QF8
10 Lux 50–100 Kohm Photoresistor	At least 2	Adafruit	161
		Amazon ASIN	B01N7V536K
TMP36 Temperature Sensor	1	Adafruit	165
		Amazon ASIN	B01GH32AQU
MPU6050 Accelerometer and Gyroscope	1	Adafruit	3886
		Amazon ASIN	B00LP25V1A
4 Channel Logic Level Converter	2	Adafruit	757
		Amazon ASIN	B07LG646VS
CP2102 or CP2104 USB-UART Converter	1	Adafruit	3309
		Amazon ASIN	B07D6LLX19
Nokia 5110 GLCD	1	Adafruit	338
		Amazon ASIN	B01EE4VQYG

(*continued*)

Table 1-2. (*continued*)

Item	Quantity	Vendor	Product Number
SSD1306 OLED	1	Adafruit	326
		Amazon ASIN	B076PDVFQD
6V Hobby DC Motor Size 130	1	Adafruit	711
		Amazon ASIN	B07BHHP2BT
Micro Servo Motor MG90S or SG92R	1	Adafruit	169
		Amazon ASIN	B07NV476P7
5V 500mA Stepper Motor	1	Jameco Electronics	237825
		Amazon ASIN	B00B88DHQ2
ULN2003 Darlington Arrays	1	Digikey Electronics	497-2344-5-ND
		Amazon ASIN	B07YSS1MQL
L293D Quadruple Half-H Drivers	1	Adafruit	807
		Amazon ASIN	B00NAY2URO
DHT11 Temperature and Humidity Sensor	1	Adafruit	386
		Amazon ASIN	B01HA8ZMWK
Common Anode RGB LED (Preferably Diffused)	1	Adafruit	159
		Amazon ASIN	B0194Y6MW2
HC-SR04 Ultrasonic Sensor	1	Adafruit	3942
		Amazon ASIN	B004U8TOE6
Piezo Speaker	1	Adafruit	160
		Amazon ASIN	B01GJLE5BS

(*continued*)

Table 1-2. (*continued*)

Item	Quantity	Vendor	Product Number
1N4001 General-Purpose Silicon Diode	1	Adafruit Amazon ASIN	755 B0087YKE02
400 Tie Points Solderless Breadboard	2	Adafruit Amazon ASIN	64 B07PCJP9DY
Jumper Wires Male to Male	At least 20	Adafruit Amazon ASIN	4482 B07GJLH7V1
Lab Bench Power Supply	1	Amazon ASIN Assorted Manufacturers	B081SFKW2R

Regarding the power supply, a high-quality 1 amp wall adapter can work as the bare minimum requirement for getting through this book. (Avoid cheap 1A adapters, as many times they are noisy and interfere with proper circuit operation.) If you plan on working with microcontrollers for a long time, however, a more substantial lab bench power supply is a good investment. This is especially important when working with motors, as they draw a lot of power when they are starting up. A standard is to use a 30V 5A lab bench power supply, like the one suggested in Table 1-2. These power supplies can handle almost anything you throw at them.

The Mu Editor

Now that we have the hardware covered, we can set up the software required for the exercises in this book. The best way to program devices using CircuitPython is with the Mu editor, which is compatible with Windows, macOS, and Linux machines. You can download the editor from *https://codewith.mu/*.

After you have downloaded and installed the Mu editor, connect your CircuitPython device to your computer with a USB cable (yes, it's that simple!) and open up Mu. You will see a window similar to Figure 1-7.

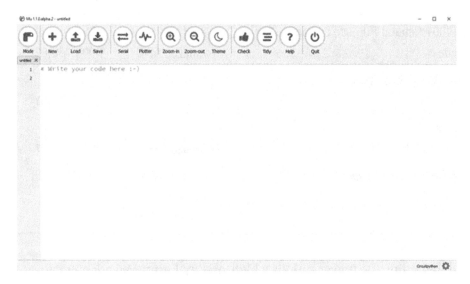

Figure 1-7. *The Mu Editor*

If your CircuitPython device is connected, you will be able to read the file on the device (this file is part of core CircuitPython). Once CircuitPython is present on the connected device, the code.py file will be present on the device once you plug it in. If your selected board does not contain CircuitPython, you can follow this guide at `https://learn.adafruit.com/installing-circuitpython-on-samd21-boards/overview`. Click the **Load** button on the editor, as seen in Figure 1-8.

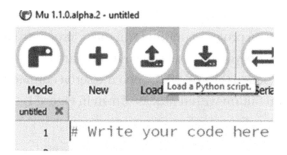

Figure 1-8. *The Load Button in Mu*

A dialog box will appear. Mu will default to the directory of the file, but in the event it does not, navigate to the drive (CircuitPython shows up just like a USB flash drive) of your CircuitPython device. You will see a *code.py* file, as is shown in Figure 1-9. The *.py* extension indicates that this is a Python code file.

Name	Date modified	Type
.fseventsd	12/4/2016 12:18 AM	File folder
lib	12/4/2016 12:18 AM	File folder
code.py	12/4/2016 12:18 AM	PY File

CIRCUITPY (E:) >   Search CIRCUITPY (E:)

Figure 1-9. *Loading the code.py File in Mu*

Open the file and you will see it contains a single line of code: `print('Hello world!')`. When a normal computer runs the `print` command, the message contained in the parentheses is displayed in a terminal, a window where you can enter commands and view the output of your code. However, your microcontroller doesn't have display capabilities or a built-in terminal window. Fortunately, CircuitPython devices by default allow communication with the host computer via a serial communication protocol. Mu has a feature called the serial monitor that allows you to see program output from the microcontroller. It will also alert you to any errors you may have in your program.

Once you've loaded the code file, open the serial connection by clicking the **Serial** button within Mu, as shown in Figure 1-10.

Figure 1-10. *The Serial Button in Mu*

Once you click the button, a small terminal window should pop up beneath the editor. This displays the serial output from the microcontroller. It should look similar to Figure 1-11.

```
CircuitPython REPL
Auto-reload is on. Simply save files over USB to run them or enter REPL to disable.

Press any key to enter the REPL. Use CTRL-D to reload.|
```

Figure 1-11. *The Serial Output Window*

Click the **Save** button in the editor, and you will observe that the print statement executed and is running in the serial output window. Your output should look similar to Figure 1-12.

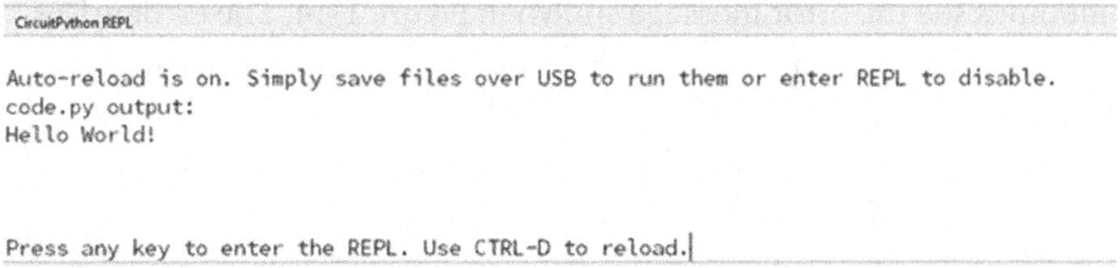

```
CircuitPython REPL

Auto-reload is on. Simply save files over USB to run them or enter REPL to disable.
code.py output:
Hello World!



Press any key to enter the REPL. Use CTRL-D to reload.|
```

Figure 1-12. *Running code.py in the Serial Output Window*

The serial terminal has some useful features. Pressing CTRL-C (or COMMAND-C for Mac) will open a Read-Evaluate-Print Loop (REPL), indicated by the >>> symbol on the screen, as shown at the bottom of Figure 1-13.

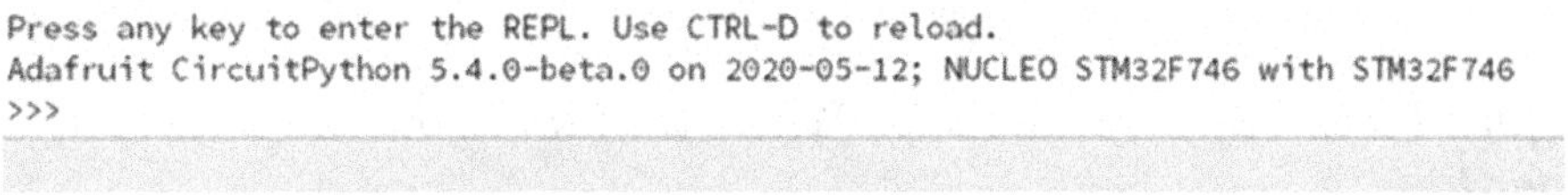

```
Press any key to enter the REPL. Use CTRL-D to reload.
Adafruit CircuitPython 5.4.0-beta.0 on 2020-05-12; NUCLEO STM32F746 with STM32F746
>>>
```

Figure 1-13. *Opening a CircuitPython REPL in the Serial Terminal*

The REPL allows you to enter your Python code line by line and have your microcontroller execute it. When you are learning how to program in a new language, sometimes you just want to try things quickly. The REPL is useful because it provides an avenue for you to easily test short snippets of code without having to resort to writing an entire program. When you open the REPL, the microcontroller stops executing the program it was running. To leave the REPL and get the program running again, press CTRL-D.

Other Serial Communication Tools

There are other tools besides Mu's serial terminal that allow you to communicate with a development board via a serial connection. These other tools will be particularly useful if you are using a custom board or if Mu has a problem detecting the board. In these cases, you will sometimes see the error message shown in Figure 1-14. The error arises when Mu is unable to find an attached board that it recognizes to work with the serial port.

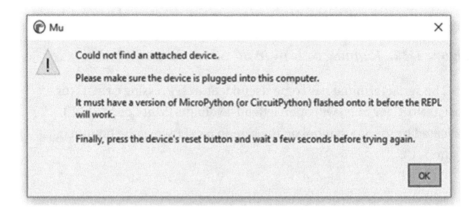

Figure 1-14. *The Error Message When Mu Can't Find the Attached Board*

If you are using a macOS or Unix computer, you can look at programs such as CoolTerm, available for download at *http://freeware.the-meiers.org/*. You can find a nice CoolTerm tutorial for macOS users at *www.mac-usb-serial.com/docs/tutorials/access-serial-port-on-mac-with-coolterm.html#*. Note that on newer versions of macOS, there may be issues running the program since the developer is not verified. To counteract this problem, open the terminal and type sudo spctl -master-disable, which will allow you to run apps downloaded from anywhere.

Windows users can also use a program called PuTTY to establish a serial connection with a development board if they have problems using the serial terminal from within Mu. It's available for download at *www.chiark.greenend.org.uk/~sgtatham/putty/*. PuTTY allows computers to communicate with each other with protocols such as Telnet and SSH. PuTTY can also communicate with virtual devices connected to the COM port on your computer. Although we are using a USB cable to connect our CircuitPython device to our computer, the device shows up as a serial port to the computer. When a USB device is emulated as a serial COM port, we call this a virtual COM port (VCP), and programs such as PuTTY allow us to read information from this VCP just as if it were an actual serial port.

Once PuTTY is downloaded and installed, on your Windows computer, go to the Control Panel and open your Device Manager. Look for your device under "Ports," as shown in Figure 1-15. Take note of the port number associated with your board.

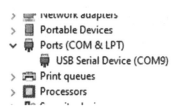

Figure 1-15. *COM Port Device*

Now you can use PuTTY to open a serial communication with your board. To do this, when you open PuTTY, set the connection type to **Serial** using the radio button. Enter the port (in our example, **COM9**) in the **Serial line** box, set the **Speed** to **115200**, then press **Open**. This is shown in Figure 1-16.

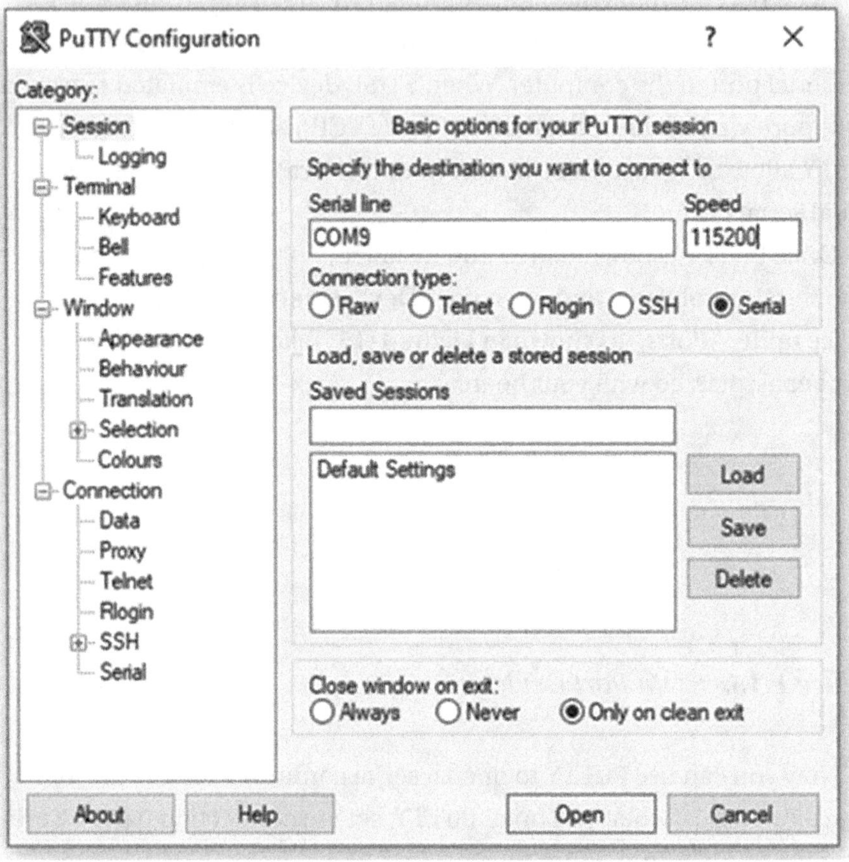

Figure 1-16. *Opening a Serial Communication with PuTTY*

PuTTY allows you to interact with your microcontroller in the same way that you interact with it from the serial terminal within Mu. Once a serial connection has been established between PuTTY and the microcontroller, you will see the output as shown in Figure 1-17. PuTTY also allows you to access the REPL.

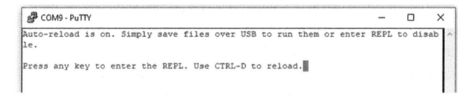

Figure 1-17. A Successful Connection in PuTTY

The options outlined in this section are all alternatives for when Mu is unable to establish a serial connection with your board. If you can connect with your board from within Mu, however, I recommend doing so, as it is a more convenient approach.

Setting Up Your Own Board

Note   This section is intended for readers who already have experience using microcontrollers, like the Arduino platform, but if you just got an Arduino Zero and want to follow along, then you can do so!

A nice feature of open source is that it is possible to build your own copy of devices without worrying about any repercussions. The CircuitPython project, for instance, has roots in the MicroPython project and has a very permissive MIT license. This license means you can do almost anything you want with CircuitPython, including compiling the source code and running it for yourself. You can also build your own hardware development board and program it with CircuitPython.

While creating a custom board is not recommended for people new to microcontrollers, this option offers many benefits to users with more experience. Setting up your own board gives you great flexibility, especially if you want to develop your own commercial product. Building your own device is also much cheaper than buying a premade board. If you are designing a finished product, for example, you wouldn't place an entire Arduino Zero or Metro M0 board into the device. Rather, you would have a printed circuit board (PCB) designed around a standard microcontroller.

If you wish to set up your own CircuitPython board, the best microcontroller to target is the SAMD21G18A microcontroller from Microchip Technology. This microcontroller is well supported by CircuitPython and will be the easiest to get going. There are two ways to load CircuitPython onto your own board. The first is to use the Arduino IDE, and the other is to use Atmel Studio. I will focus on the Arduino IDE method, since it is simpler and easier to set up. Additionally, Atmel Studio only runs on Windows devices, so the Arduino IDE method may be the only way to work on a macOS or Linux machine.

The first thing you'll need to do is load the Arduino Zero bootloader from the Arduino IDE. It is best to use the Atmel-ICE programmer to do this. Once you have connected your ISP to your target, open the Arduino IDE, go to **Tools ➤ Programmer**, and choose **Atmel-ICE**, as shown in Figure 1-18. Make sure you have an LED connected to PIN PA17 and the reset circuit is set up.

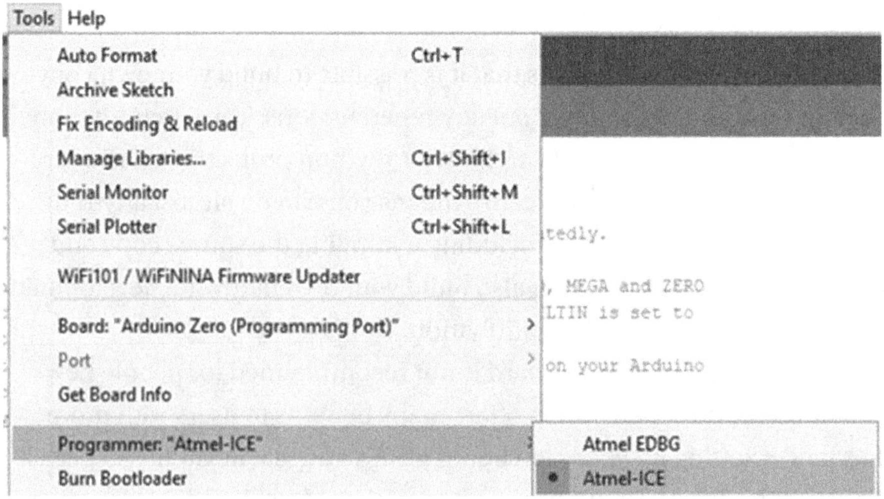

Figure 1-18. *Selecting the Programmer in Arduino IDE*

After you have selected your programmer, set the **Board** to **Arduino Zero (Programming Port)**, as in Figure 1-19.

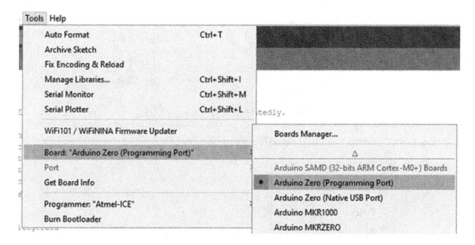

Figure 1-19. *Selecting the Board in Arduino IDE*

Then burn the bootloader by selecting **Burn Bootloader**, as shown in Figure 1-20.

Figure 1-20. *Burning the Bootloader in Arduino IDE*

After you have finished burning the bootloader, run an example sketch by selecting **File ➤ Examples ➤ Basics ➤ Blink**. Make sure the LED connected to PA17 is blinking.

The next step is to load the USB Flashing Format (UF2) bootloader. This bootloader allows the microcontroller to show up as a mass storage device so you can load and run CircuitPython on the board.

Next, head over to the CircuitPython website and grab the UF2 file for the Arduino Zero at *https://circuitpython.org/board/arduino_zero/*. The page should look similar to the one in Figure 1-21. Hit the **Download .UF2 Now** button and take note of where you save the file.

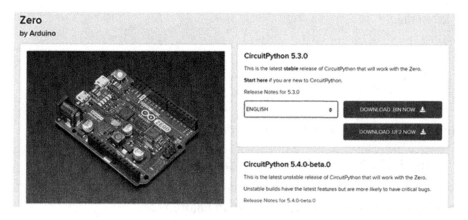

Figure 1-21. *Downloading the CircuitPython UF2 File*

Once you have downloaded this file, go to *https://github.com/ adafruit/uf2-samdx1/releases* to download the latest version of the sketch to update the bootloader of the Zero. You will see something like Figure 1-22. The file should have a name like *update-bootloader- zero-v3-10-0.ino*, though the version number may be different.

📄 update-bootloader-zero-v3.10.0.ino	53.5 KB
📄 update-bootloader-zero-v3.10.0.uf2	19.5 KB

Figure 1-22. *Download the Arduino Sketch*

Open the sketch and run it. When this is completed, connect a USB cable to your microcontroller. Pin 34 is D+ and Pin 33 is D-. Make sure to also connect the ground connection on your device. The microcontroller should now show up as a removable storage device on your computer, with the contents like Figure 1-23.

> ZEROBOOT (E:)

Name	Date modified	Type	Size
CURRENT.UF2	12/25/2018 12:00 AM	UF2 File	512 KB
INDEX.HTM	12/25/2018 12:00 AM	Chrome HTML Do...	1 KB
INFO_UF2.TXT	12/25/2018 12:00 AM	Text Document	1 KB

Figure 1-23. *The CircuitPython Device After UF2 Boot Is Successful*

Copy the UF2 file we downloaded earlier from the CircuitPython website onto the device. When it is finished copying, the device will show up as a CircuitPython device, as shown in Figure 1-24.

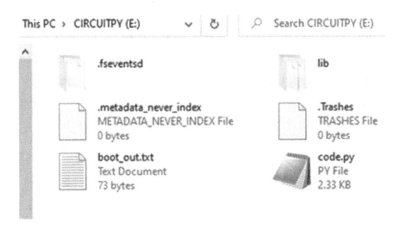

This PC > CIRCUITPY (E:)   Search CIRCUITPY (E:)

.fseventsd   lib

.metadata_never_index   .Trashes
METADATA_NEVER_INDEX File   TRASHES File
0 bytes   0 bytes

boot_out.txt   code.py
Text Document   PY File
73 bytes   2.33 KB

Figure 1-24. *The Files That Should Be Present Once CircuitPython Is Running on the Device*

Your device can now run CircuitPython. At the time of writing, the Mu editor does not recognize devices that had CircuitPython installed this way, so you will need to use PuTTY to see the output from your device on Windows or the Terminal or CoolTerm if you are using a macOS device.

For reference, Figure 1-25 shows the pinout of an Arduino Zero–based device equivalent to the custom SAMD21G18A device we just set up. You'll need to refer to this image if you're using a custom device. It shows all the digital pins, analog pins, communications, and programming interface.

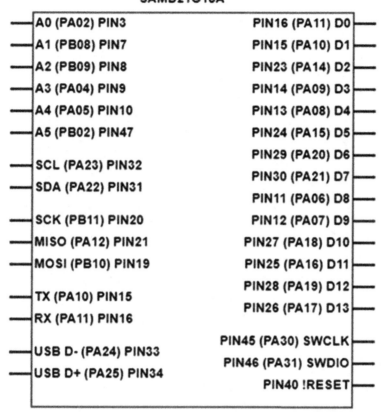

Figure 1-25. *Pinout for a Custom Arduino Zero-Based Device*

Conclusion

In this chapter, we covered the basics of microcontrollers and looked at what we need to set up our development environment. Once you have gone through the steps in this chapter, your environment should be ready for programming your microcontroller with Python. However, having a basic understanding of electronics will help you more effectively use microcontrollers to build your own devices. We will cover this topic in the next chapter.

CHAPTER 2

Electronics Primer

In the last chapter, we covered the basics of microcontrollers and how to set up a development environment. To really use microcontrollers, however, we need to interface them to the outside world. This will require a basic understanding of electronics. While it would be impossible to fully cover this vast and complicated field in a single chapter, let alone an entire book, this chapter provides an introduction to the principles of electronics and an overview of some of the components you'll be using with your microcontroller.

Electronics can be split into two main areas: analog electronics and digital electronics. Analog electronics deals with electronics in which the components within the circuit can have several states; thus, we say that analog electronics deals with continuous circuits. Digital circuits on the other hand have two states, and thus digital electronics deals with discrete circuits. In this chapter, I will discuss both.

Electricity is all about the flow of electrons. To understand electrons, let's talk about the atom a bit. The atom is said to be the smallest part of matter that can exist, and this is all good except it does not stop there. Even within the atom, there exists a myriad of subatomic particles that are described as a zoo of particles. We have protons, neutrons, electrons, quarks, mesons, and the list can go on and on.

Subatomic physics could take a lifetime to study. We will skip the complexities of that and describe the atom as being composed of three main particles. These are the proton, the neutron, and the electron. The

A. Subero, *Programming Microcontrollers with Python*,
https://doi.org/10.1007/978-1-4842-7058-5_2

proton is said to be positively charged, the neutron has no charge, and the electron has a negative charge.

Now that we have these particles in our head, one would think that they are all the same size. However, this is not so. Protons and neutrons are much larger than electrons. Something else to remember about these particles is that they are not randomly distributed in the atom. The neutrons and protons are clumped together in the center of the atom, and the electrons surround it.

This flow of electrons is called a *current*. These electrons flow for one simple reason; the conductors themselves are made of atoms. When we apply a voltage, which is a potential difference across two points of the conductor, it causes these electrons to flow as what is known as a current. Now, remember that the atoms of the conductor already have electrons; hence, when you cause more electrons to flow through the conductor, it causes an individual atom to essentially "toss out" electrons to their neighbor, and this process continues many, many times over at the speed of light.

So, let us recap for those of you who are still confused. Atoms are made up of things called protons, neutrons, and electrons. These electrons can flow through materials called conductors that allow them to flow and cannot flow through insulators which do not allow them to flow. When these electrons flow, they produce a current, and they flow because a potential difference also known as a voltage exists across the conductor. A substance that allows a current to flow through it is called a *conductor*, while a substance that does not is called an *insulator*. In order to flow, the current needs a closed path or loop, called a *circuit*.

A device called a *power source* has a potential difference across its terminals that can allow an electrical current to flow. In a paragraph above we talked about voltage which is the potential difference that causes a current to flow through objects. This potential difference does not come from itself however; it comes from a device that generates the electricity we need to power electronics. Cells and batteries are two such sources of electricity.

Anyone born within this era is sure to have encountered a battery in one form or another. Did you ever think about what a battery is? I mean you know there is one in your phone and in gadgets you have laying around. However, did you give any thought into what a battery is?

A battery is a device that we use to generate electricity and is made up of a collection of cells. Though we call everything that provides electrical power batteries, this is not the case. A cell is the single unit that produces power. A battery is formed when we have a collection of cells.

A primary cell is a cell in which the chemical reaction that took place to generate the electricity is not easily reversed. How many times have you replaced cells from clocks and remote controls around your home? Once a primary cell is depleted, it is meant to be discarded.

The alkaline cells you use to power your toys and gadgets are typically primary cells. When that AA or AAA cell dies, you toss it away and put in a new one, as is the intended use.

If we look at the cell, we will see two markings. The positive end of your power source is called the anode, and you see it marked with a little cross symbol (+). The negative end of your power source is called the cathode, and you see it marked with a little dash symbol (-). This cathode is sometimes called the ground connection.

While primary cells have their uses, our shift toward "going green" as well as advances in battery technology has led us toward using cells that can be recharged after the energy within them has been depleted. We call these cells secondary cells.

A secondary cell is a cell in which the chemical reaction that produced the electricity can be reversed. Think about it; if the chemical reaction produced electricity, should not adding electricity be able to reverse the chemical reaction that generated the electricity?

This is the premise the secondary cell operates under. Thanks to its battery chemistry, it can be recharged. These types of cells are common in our modern electronic gadgets such as our phones and tablet computers.

The electronic components we'll use throughout this book have different physical properties that allow electrons to flow through them in a certain way. When we work with these components, all we're doing is taking advantage of these properties to produce certain desirable effects. In this chapter, I'll discuss each component in turn to show how it can influence the flow of electricity.

Electrical Wires

Electrical wires are the medium by which current flows in a circuit. Wires consist of insulation surrounding a conductive metallic core. This core can be solid or stranded. Solid core wire consists of a single piece of metal at the core. Figure 2-1 shows a solid core wire beneath the insulation.

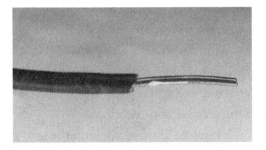

Figure 2-1. *Solid Core Wire*

Stranded core wires consist of many pieces of solid wire bundled together. Figure 2-2 shows us what stranded core wire looks like.

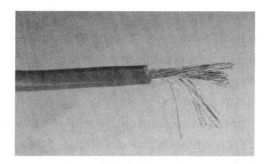

Figure 2-2. *Stranded Core Wire*

Stranded wires and solid core wires both have their applications. Solid core wire is very robust when it comes to resisting corrosions, and for applications where corrosion might occur, they are the preferred wire type. Stranded wire on the other hand is more flexible and is thus used in applications where there might be a lot of flexing of the wire. Solid core wire is more prone to breaking under a lot of flexing and is not good for such applications.

As you gain more experience, you will be able to determine which wire is suitable for which application. Sometimes, other factors such as cost or current handling capability may determine which type of wire you will use for your application.

Another important thing to know about wires is related to their size. The name we use to refer to the size of the wire is the gauge of the wire. The American Wire Gauge (AWG) is the standard most people use when they are dealing with wire sizes.

Something that always confuses beginners is related to the size of the wire and the number assigned to their gauge. In the AWG system, the larger the number is, the thinner the wire is. What this means is that a gauge 12 wire (common size for household wiring) is thicker than gauge 22 wire commonly found in electronics work.

Thicker wire generally means greater handling capability. When it comes to a comparison of wires, at DC voltages, a single core wire generally offers a higher current rating than a corresponding stranded wire with the same cross-sectional area. The reason is simple: it all boils down to heat.

The ability of a wire to handle current depends on how well it can remove the heat that is generated when a current is flowing through it. A single core wire simply must dissipate heat from the wire to the outside which is better than stranded wire. Think about the strand in the center of the stranded wire. The heat must go from this central strand and depend on other strands to conduct heat to the outside of the wire which leads to poorer heat dissipation.

The Breadboard

As we begin to work with electronic components, we'll need a surface where we can build our circuits. We call this surface a *breadboard*. A breadboard is a board that consists of little holes called sockets where we can attach our components. Figure 2-3 shows a breadboard.

Figure 2-3. *A Breadboard*

A breadboard's sockets are arranged into groups. On either side of the board are vertical strips of sockets called the power terminals, power rails, or power bus. These are marked with a plus "+" sign used to indicate where the positive connection to the power supply goes and with a negative "–" sign used to indicate where the ground connection on the circuit is connected. Inside the breadboard, all the sockets in a single + or – column are connected with a metal wire, allowing electricity to flow between the sockets. The power rails are seen in Figure 2-4.

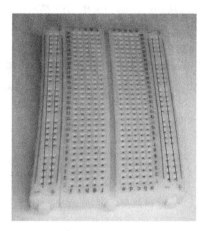

Figure 2-4. *The Breadboard's Power Rails Are Highlighted with Red Lines*

The center of the breadboard consists of strips of sockets that are organized into rows. This part of the breadboard is called the prototyping area. Each row has two groups of five sockets, separated by a trench that runs down the middle. Each row of sockets is given a number; on our example breadboard, they are numbered from 1 to 30. There are also letters assigned to each socket within a row. Inside the breadboard, each group of five sockets is connected with a metal wire, as is highlighted in Figure 2-5. The central trench is used for supporting components called integrated circuits, which will be discussed later on in the chapter.

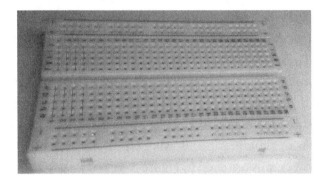

Figure 2-5. *The Prototyping Area, with the First Few Rows of Sockets Highlighted in Red*

Male-to-male jumper wires, such as the one shown in Figure 2-6, have connectors that can easily fit into the sockets of a breadboard.

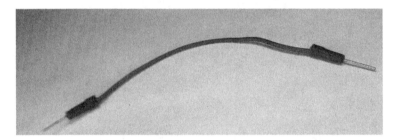

Figure 2-6. *Jumper Wire*

These jumper wires are used to connect different sockets together, providing a path for a current to flow through the components on the breadboard.

Electronic Schematics

When describing electronics, it is customary to use a *schematic diagram* to represent the circuit you are working with. Imagine we have a motor connected to a battery, as shown in Figure 2-7.

Figure 2-7. *A Simple Circuit Featuring a Motor Connected to a Battery*

You can replace the pictorial representation of circuit components with special electronic representations of them. The representation is called a schematic. In our first circuit, we connected a battery to a motor. Figure 2-8 shows us how we can redraw this circuit as a pictorial representation. This pictorial representation of the circuit is called a circuit diagram. In a circuit diagram, we use graphics to represent our electrical circuit.

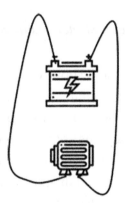

Figure 2-8. *Pictorial Representation of Our Circuit*

The circuit in Figure 2-8 can be redrawn with special symbols to represent the components that make up the circuit, as shown in Figure 2-9. This is because while circuit diagrams are great, as our circuits become more complex, it becomes harder to adequately use circuit diagrams to represent our circuits. The diagram in Figure 2-9 uses schematic symbols to represent our circuit. The schematic diagram uses abstract graphic symbols to represent elements within a circuit rather than pictorial representations.

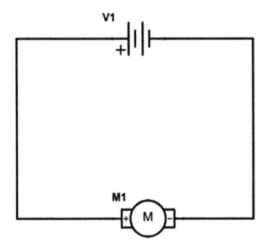

Figure 2-9. *The Same Circuit Shown Using Schematic Symbols*

These terms are not set in stone however, as some people refer to circuit diagrams as schematic diagrams in some instances. However, you should be aware that a difference in how we represent our circuits exists. In this book, I use schematic diagrams as they are clearer and more concise than circuit diagrams. Also, once you understand schematic diagrams, you should be able to understand circuit diagrams without any problem.

Every component we use in electronics has its own standardized schematic symbol used to represent it. Here are the symbols for the components we have used thus far.

The wire is represented by a straight line, as shown in Figure 2-10. The rows and columns of connected holes in the breadboard can be thought of as wires since they allow the components within the circuit to be connected.

Figure 2-10. *Wire Schematic Symbol*

A cell is represented by one short line and one long line parallel to each other with wires coming out the sides as is shown in Figure 2-11.

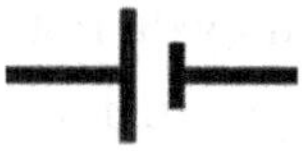

Figure 2-11. *Cell Schematic Symbol*

The schematic symbol for a battery is several cells joined as is shown in Figure 2-12.

Figure 2-12. *Battery Schematic Symbol*

The motor also has its own schematic symbol which is a circle with a capital M on the inside which is depicted in Figure 2-13.

Figure 2-13. *Motor Schematic Symbol*

There are many more schematic symbols that will be gradually introduced as we move along.

Passive Components

We are now ready to cover what are known as *passive components*. They are called passive because they do not require any external source of power in order to operate. These are devices that are capable of dissipating, storing, and releasing electrical power. Passive components include *resistors*, *capacitors*, and *inductors*.

Resistors

A resistor is a device that resists the flow of electrons through it. This is needed to limit the current that flows into certain circuit components. If we put too much current into some components, they will be damaged, and for that reason, we use resistors to prevent this from happening. Resistors also form part of a particularly important circuit known as a voltage divider. A voltage divider turns a larger voltage into a smaller one which is useful when building certain circuits, as we will see later in this book.

We measure the amount of resistance in a substance with a unit known as ohms. When we really think about it, all resistance is is a relationship between voltage and current in a circuit. Essentially, it is a ratio of voltage across a substance to the current through it. This relationship forms something known as Ohm's law.

We cannot talk about circuits without discussing Ohm's law. A guy named Georg Ohm developed a law, and in this law, he found a relationship between voltage, resistance, and current.

Voltage = Current * Resistance

This relationship is simple but powerful! To illustrate this, let us say we have a voltage of 5 volts flowing in your circuit and a resistor with a value of 1k.

How do we calculate the current? Well, we simply rearrange Ohm's law and get the following:

Current = Voltage / Resistance

So, we can calculate the current in the circuit to be 5v / 1000 ohm = 0.5 milliamps.

In Figure 2-14, we see what a few resistors look like.

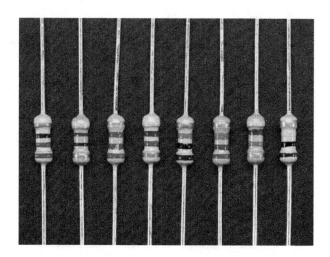

Figure 2-14. *Some ResistorsCredit: Adafruit, adafruit.com*

Resistors come with colored bands printed on them to indicate the value of the resistor. The first band indicates the first digit of the resistor, the second band the second digit, and the third band the number of zeros.

The fourth band is called the tolerance level of the resistor, and it tells us what percentage of the original value the resistor may be over or under by. We read these resistor color codes from left to right; then according to the color of the band, we assign values based on the number of bands the resistor has. We can usually tell which band is the first band by looking for the gold or silver tolerance band on the resistor; the tolerance band will be the rightmost band, so we look at the leftmost band to start determining the value. Usually, the tolerance band will have a small gap between it and the value bands, but this is not always the case. Table 2-1 has the list of colors we can use to determine the value of the resistor.

Table 2-1. Resistor Color Codes

Color	Number
Black	0
Brown	1
Red	2
Orange	3
Yellow	4
Green	5
Blue	6
Violet	7
Gray	8
White	9

The tolerance band may be brown to indicate a 1% tolerance, gold to indicate a 5% tolerance, silver to indicate a 10% tolerance, or no stripe at all may indicate a 20% tolerance. There are other bands that indicate other tolerance levels, but these are the ones you will most frequently encounter.

Resistors are a very well-behaved component. Rarely do you have a problem with a circuit in which resistors are the culprit. If resistors fail within a circuit, it's either because of a poor design choice or the failure of another component that takes the resistor down with it.

The schematic symbol for the resistor is a jagged line, as is shown in Figure 2-15.

Figure 2-15. *The Resistor Schematic Symbol*

Capacitors

Capacitors are responsible for storing electrical energy within a circuit. One of the most common uses for them is in filter circuits together with resistors. Filters in electronics are used to allow certain frequencies of electrical signals to pass through them while attenuating or reducing others. Some types of filters are even able to amplify or modify signals of the frequencies they allow to pass.

Filter circuits have many important applications; one such application is in audio signals when you want to create a two-way crossover circuit and direct all the high frequencies to a tweeter while attenuating low frequency signals.

The characteristics of capacitors are dependent on the material of which they are made; we call the material they are made from the dielectric. The dielectric will determine whether the capacitor is polarized or non-polarized. A polarized capacitor must be connected a certain way within a circuit; otherwise, it will be damaged and presents a fire hazard. Non-polarized capacitors can be connected either way in a circuit without problems.

51

The amount of charge a capacitor can hold, called its capacitance, is measured in a unit known as the farad. One farad is a large amount of storage, and for that reason, we usually use capacitors in small amounts, usually microfarads (μF) and picofarads (pF) – one-millionth and one-trillionth of a farad, respectively.

Some things to look out for when working with capacitors are their temperature range and their working voltage. These values are often printed on the body of the device. The temperature range represents the minimum and maximum temperatures at which the capacitor will function correctly, while the working voltage is the maximum voltage that can be fed into the capacitor. It is important not to exceed the working voltage, as it will cause damage to the device. When capacitors fail, they burn, and they have the capability to take along other circuit components with them.

If the capacitor does not have a voltage or temperature rating printed on it, it is best to consult the datasheet for your device. This is a document that lists all the characteristics of the device you are using, including safe operating voltages and recommended operating temperatures.

Polarized Capacitors

The most common polarized capacitor you are likely to encounter is the aluminum electrolytic capacitor, as is shown in Figure 2-16. These capacitors feature large capacitance when compared to most non-polarized capacitors.

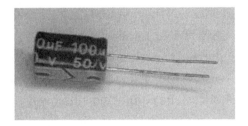

Figure 2-16. *An Aluminum Electrolytic Capacitor*

Due to their construction, aluminum electrolytic capacitors suffer from a problem known as leakage current. Leakage current occurs because the insulator in the capacitor is not perfect, and thus some current does flow through it. To counteract this problem, another capacitor known as the tantalum electrolytic capacitor was created which has much lower leakage current than their aluminum counterparts.

Non-polarized Capacitors

Ceramic capacitors are by far the most encountered non-polarized capacitor you will use. Figure 2-17 shows what a ceramic capacitor looks like.

Figure 2-17. *A Ceramic Capacitor*

Ceramic capacitors offer higher working voltages than aluminum electrolytic capacitors, though their capacitance is much lower. Typically, you would select one or the other based on your capacitance requirements. If you need a large capacitance, then you would use electrolytic capacitors; however, if you want a small capacitance, you will tend to use ceramic capacitors.

If you look at the ceramic capacitor, you will observe three numbers printed on them. The first two digits represent the value of the capacitor, and the last digit gives us the multiplier. All we do is take the first two digits and add the number of zeros specified in the multiplier. This gives the resulting capacitance in picofarads. If you do not see any third digit, then that is the value in picofarads. So, if you see a capacitor with just "10" written, the value of the capacitor is 10 picofarads.

For example, the capacitor listed in Figure 2-17 has a marking of 104. So, the value will be 10 + 0000 which is 100 000 pF or 0.1uF.

Capacitor Schematic Symbols

Figure 2-18 shows us how polarized capacitors are represented with schematic symbols, and Figure 2-19 shows us how non-polarized capacitors are represented.

Figure 2-18. *Polarized Capacitor Schematic Symbols*

Figure 2-19. *Non-polarized Capacitor Schematic Symbols*

The polarized capacitor always has one lead with a plus "+" symbol next to it. Non-polarized capacitors do not have any polarization markings.

Inductors

Inductors are an especially important component that I think too many people make overcomplicated. You can learn about inductors with the use of calculus and other advanced mathematics, or you can look at inductors from the standpoint of what they are, just another component to use. Do not worry; we will cover inductors and their uses in the most practical way possible throughout this book.

Before we get more into inductors, we must understand electromagnetism. At one point or another in our life, we would have encountered magnets.

Magnets are materials that exhibit magnetism. This is to say magnets are materials that exhibit the properties of having a magnetic field. When we have the flow of a current through a conductor, we have a magnetic field that is generated. If we have a piece of wire with current flowing through it, the magnetic field will be very weak. If that wire is wrapped into a coil, a stronger magnetic field is created, and this forms the basis for an electromagnet.

A coil of wire would produce a magnetic field. However, this would still be a very weak field. We can increase the strength of the magnetic field by increasing the number of turns of wire on the coil.

To cause a large increase in the strength of the magnetic field, we introduce a material that is magnetically permeable into the core of the coil. This material is usually iron. When we do this, we now get a strong magnet that can be controlled electronically. A coil with a magnetically permeable core is called a solenoid.

We just learned about capacitors and that they can store electric charge, and we also learned that electromagnetism is the process whereby a conductor when it has an electric field running through it causes that conductor to form a magnetic field.

Inductors are devices which store electric charge. That coiled up wire we were talking about is an inductor, and for that reason, you may sometimes hear persons refer to inductors as coils.

The difference between inductors and capacitors is that inductors store their electric charge as a magnetic field. As far as the operation of the inductor goes, you can design a lot of circuits by treating the inductor as just that, a black box that stores electric charge in a magnetic field.

Inductance abbreviated (L) is measured in henries (H).

Inductors come in a vast array of packages that have different purposes. These inductors may be either shielded or unshielded. Remember we spoke about electromagnetism? Well, an inductor due to its design generates a magnetic field. This magnetic field can have undesirable effects on surrounding electronic circuits. We can design the inductor in a way that is shielded so that it will minimize the effects of interference on the environment.

Inductors are used for blocking high-frequency noise on power lines; for this reason, we call inductors used like this chokes. These are commonly found in power circuits such as inverters and motor control circuits. These chokes can be built to handle rather high current. They are also used in designing electronic filters similar to the capacitor.

For a long time, "air core" inductors had widespread use. These inductors were formed by simply taking a solid core wire and winding it into a coil. Though these still have their applications, there are limitations to such inductors. You can achieve greater inductance in a smaller package by simply adding an iron core for the wire to coil around. Over time, other core materials and designs became common. As such, modern inductors look different than just having a coil of wire with an iron bar in the center. Figure 2-20 shows one type of inductor you are likely to encounter in modern electronics along with its schematic symbol on the left.

Figure 2-20. *An Inductor and Its Schematic Symbol*

Technology has so much advanced that a compact class of inductors called planar inductors exists. These have a remarkably high current handling capability considering their small size.

Semiconductors

In the last section, the resistors, capacitors, and inductors we looked at are known as passive analog circuit components. There are also a class of circuit components that are known as active circuit components. We will begin our discussion on active analog circuit components with a little discussion on semiconductors. I mentioned semiconductors earlier and told you we would cover them later. This section is the fulfilment of that promise.

We learned that while some substances such as silver and copper are good conductors, others such as rubber and glass are insulators. However, there is a special class of materials that are known as semiconductors.

In electronics, the two most used semiconductor materials in components are germanium (Ge) and silicon (Si). Though in recent years some other semiconductive components you will see on the market are constructed of gallium nitride (GaN) and silicon carbide (SiC).

57

Semiconductors conduct better than insulators but conduct more poorly than conductors. Another way of thinking about semiconductors is that they have less resistance than insulators, but more resistance than conductors. These devices however only exhibit these properties under special conditions such as with temperature or addition of other materials.

Semiconductors as mentioned earlier are not the best conductors. The conductivity of these semiconductors can be increased by adding certain impurities to them so that they become either n-type semiconductors or p-type semiconductors. The adding of these impurities is a process known as doping. When these p-type and n-type semiconductors are joined, they form what is known as a pn junction.

When you apply DC voltage between two points in a circuit for a certain operation, it is known as biasing. When you apply voltage in such a way that it can flow through a pn junction, this is known as forward bias. You can achieve forward bias by connecting a power supply to a pn junction so that the positive side of the power source is connected to the positive end of the pn junction, and the negative side is connected to the negative end of the pn junction.

However, if you apply voltage in such a way that the positive terminal is connected to the negative end of a pn junction and the negative end of the terminal is connected to the positive end of the junction, you create what is known as a reverse bias. When you reverse bias a pn junction, it has a large resistance and does not allow voltage to flow.

However, you should know a tiny amount of current flows when you reverse bias a pn junction. Also, when you apply a voltage to a pn junction, it will take a voltage above a certain amount; for silicon, it is 0.7 volts, known as a voltage drop for current to start to flow in a circuit. This voltage which causes a rapid increase in current flow is known as a knee voltage. If you apply a large reverse voltage to the pn junction, it breaks down. The voltage at which the junction breaks down is known as the reverse voltage.

The peak inverse voltage is a term people use to refer to the maximum amount of reverse voltage you can apply to a pn junction before it is damaged.

Diode

The first semiconductor device we will look at is the *diode.* A diode only allows current to flow in one direction. When it is connected in that direction and current can flow, a diode is said to be forward biased. When it is connected in the other direction, a diode does not allow current to flow, and it is said to be reverse biased. Diodes are identified by a band on the cathode of the device. Figure 2-21 shows what a diode looks like.

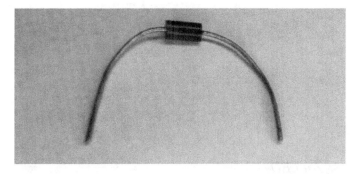

Figure 2-21. *A Diode*

The schematic symbol for a diode is a triangle with a line at the tip, as shown in Figure 2-22.

Figure 2-22. *The Diode Schematic Symbol*

Diodes have a negligible resistance when connected in the forward direction and a very high resistance when connected in the reverse direction. There are signal diodes, which are used for small current circuits, and power diodes, which can handle higher voltage and currents.

Light-Emitting Diode

The *light-emitting diode (LED)* is a special type of diode that produces light when it is forward biased. An LED can produce visible light, infrared light, or ultraviolet light. Figure 2-23 shows what a light-emitting diode looks like.

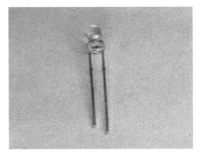

Figure 2-23. *An LED*

The LED schematic symbol is just like the diode symbol except there is a circle around it, as shown in Figure 2-24.

Figure 2-24. *LED Schematic Symbol*

LEDs, like all diodes, have a *voltage drop*. This voltage drop is dependent on the type of material the LED is manufactured from.

There are two leads on an LED. The longer of these leads is called the anode. This is where you connect the positive voltage. The shorter lead is called the cathode. This is where you put your ground connection. If we look at the LED inside the plastic case, you will see that one of the leads looks larger and flat inside the case. This can also be used to identify the cathode. Additionally, on round LEDs, the plastic casing itself has a flat edge; this is yet another way you can use to identify the LED. The reason for all these markers is the LEDs do not like to be connected the wrong way. We will discuss this later when we learn how to use the LED.

Transistor

The *transistor* is one of the most important devices ever created. It was central to allowing the computer revolution to take place.

A transistor is formed by putting either a p-type or n-type material between a pair of opposite types. Thus, when you have two n-type semiconductors with a p-type semiconductor in between, you get an N-P-N transistor. If you have two p-type semiconductors with an n-type semiconductor in between, you will get a P-N-P transistor. This NPN or PNP junction can be thought of as two diodes connected back to back, one forward biased and the other reverse biased. A transistor's name comes from the fact that it transfers the signal given to it from the low resistance diode to the high resistance one. In fact, the transistor is short for "transfer resistor."

The devices we have been discussing up to this point have one thing in common: they are all two-terminal devices. The transistor, however, has three terminals: the base, the collector, and the emitter. They are represented by the letters B, C, and E, respectively. Figure 2-25 has a diagram that shows what these transistor pins look like.

Figure 2-25. *Transistor Diagram*

When current flows into the base of a transistor, it causes a greater amount of current than the amount flowing into the base to flow from the collector to the emitter. The more current that flows at the base, the more current will flow from the collector to the emitter. We see a transistor in Figure 2-26.

Figure 2-26. *Physical Transistor*

The NPN transistor schematic symbol is given in Figure 2-27. The symbol is a circle with the three pins collector, base, and emitter labeled as C, B, and E, respectively. The NPN transistor has the arrow on the emitter pointing away from the base.

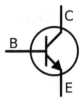

Figure 2-27. *NPN Transistor Diagram*

The PNP transistor schematic symbol is shown in Figure 2-28. The PNP transistor looks like the NPN transistor with the emitter pointing toward the base.

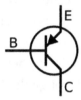

Figure 2-28. *PNP Transistor Diagram*

The point where a p-type and n-type conductor meet is called a junction. The junction where the emitter and base meet is called the emitter diode. Remember that a transistor can be thought of as two back-to-back diodes. The junction where the collector and base meet is called the collector diode. The emitter diode is forward biased which allows current to flow, and the collector diode is reverse biased as it does not allow current to flow. Keep this in mind as we move forward. The types of transistors discussed here due to this method of constructing them are known as bipolar junction transistors or BJTs.

Metal-Oxide-Semiconductor Field-Effect Transistors

A *metal-oxide-semiconductor field-effect transistor (MOSFET)* operates like a voltage-controlled resistor (VCR). These VCRs have one input port and two output ports; the input port voltage controls the resistance between the output ports. The resistance varies nonlinearly with the voltage that is input to the device. This property allows the input port to effectively turn the MOSFET on or off. When a MOSFET is on, it has a low resistance, which is in the order of a fraction of an ohm. When you look at the datasheet of a MOSFET, you will see its RDS(On) value, which is the drain to source resistance when the device is in saturation. A MOSFET is said to be in saturation when the maximum amount of gate voltage is applied to the device, which makes the RDS(On) being very small, allowing maximum drain current to flow through the MOSFET. A lower RDS(On) value means the device will run cooler and more efficiently.

We can see a MOSFET in Figure 2-29. This is a TO-220 package, which is not uncommon for MOSFETs.

Figure 2-29. *A MOSFET*

Just as BJTs come in two varieties, so too do MOSFETs come in two varieties. Figure 2-30 shows the schematic symbols for both. On the left is an N-channel MOSFET, which is like an NPN BJT, and on the right is the P-channel MOSFET, which is like a PNP BJT.

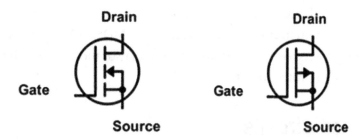

Figure 2-30. *The Schematic Symbols for N-Channel and P-Channel MOSFETs*

An important factor to consider is the gate threshold voltage which indicates the minimum voltage that is required to conduct current into the drain. Divert your attention to Figure 2-31.

Like transistors, MOSFETs have three pins. They are labeled drain, gate, and source. These are the equivalent of a transistor's collector, base, and emitter pins, respectively. Usually, you can replace your transistor with a MOSFET for most applications.

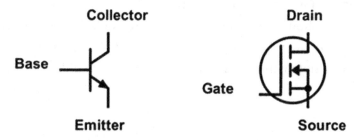

Figure 2-31. *Transistor and MOSFET Side by Side*

Some precautions for using MOSFETs are make sure to never exceed the gate to source voltage as you will damage the MOSFET. Also, when you are switching inductive loads (names we give to devices that are inductors), then ensure you are using a flyback diode (a diode connected across the device) to protect the MOSFET. This is something we will discuss in more detail later when we look at using motors with our device; for now just keep in mind that when you do use MOSFETs, if you are using a device which acts as an inductor such as a relay or motor, you will need to use a diode to protect the device.

Integrated Circuits

The devices we've looked at so far are called *discrete components* because each one only has one function. By contrast, an *integrated circuit (IC)* is a component that takes several discrete components and puts them into one device. An IC provides a lot of useful features in a compact package. By combining components we have looked at before into different circuit configurations, then we can get a desirable function for that circuit. Instead of using discrete components to achieve this function, we can make the discrete devices miniaturized and make the IC. A microcontroller, for example, as we learned in the last chapter, is a type of IC that combines many different circuit functions into one package. We will learn about different types of ICs further in the book.

Figure 2-32 shows what an integrated circuit looks like. There is usually a notch at the top to indicate which pin is the first pin on the device. If you don't see a notch, then you will see a dot which would serve the same purpose.

Figure 2-32. *Integrated Circuit Package*

The type of IC shown in Figure 2-32 is a dual inline package (DIP) IC. These ICs typically range from 4 to 40 pins and usually have the pins distributed equally on the sides of the plastic case that houses everything. The pins are usually spaced 0.1 inches apart which makes DIP ICs ideal for insertion into a breadboard.

Though DIP technology is great for prototyping, today you would find that most ICs are manufactured as surface mount technology (SMT) devices, which are made for machine assembly and allow electronics to be made easier at lower cost. SMT devices are hard to work with as a beginner, though there are adapters you can use to make them fit in a breadboard.

Digital Logic

Now that we have covered basic analog electronics, we can look at digital electronics. Analog circuit components such as transistors and diodes can be combined in different ways to make digital logic circuits. The basic building blocks of all digital electronics are the logic gates; thus, our discussion on digital logic begins with a discussion on *logic gates*. A logic gate is a circuit configuration that takes in inputs and delivers an output state of either high or low. These high and low states correspond to voltage levels. In traditional digital electronics, we consider a high to be typically 1.8, 3.3, or 5 volts and a low to be 0 volts. These high and low voltages can vary, though for most applications these are the voltage levels we will consider. Essentially, a high is what we call a logical level "1" and the low voltage we call a logical "0". This is known as a binary system. Binary systems use only two digits 0 and 1 to represent all their information. Digital logic circuits use these logic levels on their input and produce a binary output. For the digital logic circuits we look at in this section, this output is usually a single binary digit, which we call a bit.

A logic gate typically has two inputs and one output. Though it is possible to construct gates with any number of inputs, we will stick with two inputs to make things simple. Logic gates are available as discrete components that you can connect to your microcontroller (we will look at one such type in the next section), and when used like this, they are called glue logic, since they allow different logic circuits to be connected to work together by acting as a bridging interface to them. They are also encountered as larger parts of circuits, which we will see in later chapters in this book. In this section, we will look at some common logic gates.

The first logic gate we will look at is the *AND gate*. The AND gate compares two binary values. If both values are a logical 1, or HIGH, then the result is a logical 1 and the output will be HIGH. If any of the values on the input are a logical 0, or LOW, then the output of the gate will be LOW. Figure 2-33 shows the symbol for an AND gate.

Figure 2-33. *An AND Gate*

An *OR gate* compares two binary values. If either value is a logical 1, or HIGH, then the result is a logical 1 and the output will be HIGH. If both values are a logical 1, then the output will also be HIGH. If both of the values on the input are a logical 0, or LOW, then the output on the gate will be LOW. Figure 2-34 shows the symbol for an OR gate.

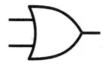

Figure 2-34. *An OR Gate*

The *NOT gate* is another gate that is frequently encountered in the world of digital electronics. It presents the opposite of its input as its output. If the input is LOW, then the output will be HIGH, and if the input is HIGH, then the output will be LOW. Figure 2-35 has the schematic symbol for a NOT gate.

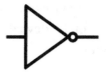

Figure 2-35. *A NOT Gate*

Another important gate is the *XOR gate*. XOR stands for eXclusive OR. The XOR gate will output a high value if the inputs have opposite values, or else the output will be low. Put another way, its output is high exclusively if one or the other input – but not both – is high. The XOR gate can use this unique ability to perform a lot of different tasks such as in parity checking (used to ensure data is transferred correctly), and a feature of an XOR gate is that any number that is XORed with itself yields a 0 which is used to clear registers in machine code (we will learn more about this later) and can be used within a microprocessor to aid with making more efficient addition. Also, if you XOR the same number twice (we perform a XOR, take its output value, then XOR it again), you get back the original value! The XOR gate symbol is shown in Figure 2-36.

Figure 2-36. *An XOR Gate*

The last gate we will look at is the *buffer gate*. A buffer gate takes an input signal and does not invert the output; if you input a logical HIGH, you get a HIGH out, and if you put a LOW in, you get a LOW out. Buffer gates are used to amplify a digital signal. If the device providing the logical signal at the input cannot sink (provide current) or source (take current in) enough current to the target (we will see this in action later on when we look at input and output with the microcontroller), a buffer gate is used to strengthen the drive capabilities of the device at its input. Figure 2-37 has the schematic symbol for a buffer.

Figure 2-37. *A Buffer*

All these logic gates have their applications as we will see going forward.

Logic Level Conversion

When working with digital logic, it is sometimes necessary to convert from one logic level (like 1.8 volts, 3.3 volts, or 5 volts) to another. This is because different devices run at different voltages. In the early days of digital circuits, it was common to have systems run at 5 volts. Since 5 volts was the standard when intelligent devices such as microprocessors came along, they also used 5-volt logic for their operation. As such, many peripherals (special circuits on the microcontroller we will learn about later) and modules are designed to work with 5-volt systems.

In recent years, however, the industry trend has been toward using 3.3-volt logic levels or even 1.8 volts. Due to the number of years that 5-volt systems have been around, sometimes it is necessary to combine lower logic levels with modules or other ICs that use 5-volt logic, as they may be more readily available or the design team may have experience with the robustness of such devices. In such a case, it may be necessary to perform logic level conversion to get from one voltage to the other. Note that if you are using a 5-volt peripheral with a 3.3-volt logic level, then you may be able to interface with the device without the need for logic level conversion. However, when using 3.3-volt logic devices with 5-volt logic levels, a converter is necessary. To be on the safe side though, you can use a logic level converter whenever you are working across different logic level domains. You would usually use dedicated ICs for this purpose. A special logic level conversion PCB like the one shown in Figure 2-38 can also be used. This logic level converter can be thought of as several buffer logic gates that do not alter the information but simply modify the drive current on the input or output.

Figure 2-38. *Logic Level Converter*

Flip-Flop

Now that we have examined discrete logic gates, we can turn to the *flip-flop*, which forms part of a computer's memory. The flip-flop is the smallest unit of memory. A flip-flop can store a single bit of data in the form of either a high or low logic state. In digital electronics, there are combinational logic circuits and sequential logic circuits. Combinational logic circuits have their outputs changed as soon as their input is modified; take the AND gate, for example, as soon as the inputs of the gates are changed; the output will change immediately in response to that input. The reason the flip-flop can be used as computer memory is that it falls into the category of a sequential logic circuit. Such circuits only change their output state if you do so intentionally, regardless of what you do on the input. This output is usually changed in response to not only the current inputs but also on the previous inputs to the device. The flip-flop is the basic building block of sequential logic circuits.

The clocked RS flip-flop is one such sequential flip-flop circuit. The clocked RS flip-flop is dependent on a clock pulse being applied to the input to change state. The JK flip-flop clears up some of the inconsistencies related to invalid conditions caused by both S and R being logical 1. The JK flip-flop is thus a popular flip-flop that is often used in digital design. In Figure 2-39, we see a JK flip-flop.

Figure 2-39. *A JK Flip-Flop*

The pin we see with the triangle on the flip-flop in between the J and K pins, which are input pins, is the clock pin; the clock pin takes a clock input. A clock can be thought of as a logic level signal that alternates between a high and low logic level state. The state when the clock transitions from low to high is called the rising edge of the clock, and the state when the clock transitions from high to low is called the falling edge of the clock. We also have output pins which are Q and !Q (not Q). If J and K are in a logical HIGH state and we apply a clock signal, then the outputs at Q and !Q will change state. If both J and K are in a LOW logical level state and we apply a clock pulse, then there will be no change on the output.

JK flip-flops are known as universal flip-flops, and they are used in devices like shift registers, pulse-width modulation (PWM) circuits, and counters, among other types of circuits we will learn about in this book.

Registers and the Shift Register

The flip-flop forms the foundation of the basic unit of computing memory. Another term we use to refer to a basic unit of computer memory is the *register*. Registers are used to store and manipulate data within the computer. Registers utilize flip-flops for data storage, and thanks to this, we can read and write from them easily. For ease of understanding, you can think of a register as a black box that stores a bit of data, and internally this black box uses a flip-flop to accomplish this task.

One type of register that you will encounter is the *shift register*. A shift register can store a sequence of either 4 or 8 bits. The shift register has a sequence of flip-flops that are connected in such a way that when a pulse of a clock is applied to the device, bits are moved from one flip-flop to the next.

To accomplish this, a shift register usually has a chain of D flip-flops. A D flip-flop can be thought of as a JK flip-flop with only one input, which makes the flip-flop easier to use; however, it requires more logic circuits to realize its implementation. Within a shift register, we call each D flip-flop a latch. The difference between a latch and a flip-flop in the strictest sense is that a latch is level triggered, whereas a flip-flop is edge triggered. What this means is that the latch is asynchronous, changing the inputs as soon as the inputs change the logic level, whereas the flip-flop depends on the state of the clock signal (using either the rising or falling edge of the clock) to change its input.

We say something is level triggered when it responds to a transition of a voltage level on the input of the device, which can be a high or low logic level. An edge-triggered device on the other hand responds to the edges of the clock signal, and it may be triggered by the rising edge or falling edge of the clock signal.

Within a shift register containing the latches, the output of one latch is connected to the input of another latch, and data can be fed into the shift register serially (one bit at a time), or it can be fed in parallel (all the bits at the same time).

Thanks to this arrangement, we can have a wide array of shift registers which are

- Serial In Serial Out (SISO)

- Serial In Parallel Out (SIPO)

- Parallel In Parallel Out (PIPO)

- Parallel In Serial Out (PISO)

- Bidirectional shift register

Each type of shift register has its own application. Today, many shift registers are integrated within ICs, so they are not frequently used as discrete components.

Multiplexers and Demultiplexers

A *multiplexer* is a digital circuit that combines two or more input lines into a single output. This is sometimes called muxing. Figure 2-40 has a multiplexer circuit.

Figure 2-40. *A Multiplexer*

The multiplexer has two inputs labeled 0 and 1 or A and B, and another input line called SEL0, as well as an output line Y. According to the value of the input lines, the multiplexer assigns a value to the output. If the selector line is low, then line 1 will be on the output. If the selector line is high, the output will reflect the value on the line 0.

A *demultiplexer* does the opposite of a multiplexer. It converts a single input into many different outputs. A demultiplexer is shown in Figure 2-41.

Figure 2-41. *A Demultiplexer*

The demultiplexer has an input A or F and two outputs 0 and 1 or A and B, as well as a selector line, SEL0. The binary pattern on the input line will be converted to values on the output lines. When the select line is low, then the input at A will be on the line 0, and when the select line is high, then the multiplexer will assign the input at A to line 1.

75

Conclusion

In this chapter, we covered basic electronics, with a focus on some of the actual components that are commonly used. We looked at passive analog devices, as well as semiconductors, diodes, transistors, and MOSFETs. We also looked at some of the components of digital electronics. Armed with the basics of digital electronics, you will better understand microcontrollers when you work with them later. I hope in this chapter you will have learned that electronics concepts build upon one another. Diodes and transistors, though they are analog components, can be combined to form digital building blocks of which microcontrollers are comprised; the knowledge learned here will seem to be abstract for now, but I assure you as we learn about the various peripherals on the microcontroller, then we will understand how useful this information is. The information here will serve you on your microcontroller journey.

CHAPTER 3

Embedded Systems Overview

As much as I would like you to just start writing code, it is imperative that we do a bit of talking so that you will understand how your code is structured. In this chapter, we cover a bit of theory of embedded systems which gives you the background you need to follow along with the rest of the book. In the last chapter, we looked at an overview of some basic electronics, and in this chapter, we look at the embedded system as a whole to better understand where microcontrollers fit into the entire scope of things. Indeed, the contents of this chapter alone can occupy a book by itself! This chapter is necessarily long and gives you principles that will last throughout your career.

An Overview of Embedded Systems

We will start our journey at the very beginning and discuss what an embedded system is. An embedded system is a system that is designed for one purpose or one function rather, which it is expected to perform with a high degree of reliability and with minimum user intervention. The defining characteristics of embedded systems are that they are usually resource constrained. What this means is that they do not usually have the gigabytes of RAM, endless electrical power, and computing power of regular computing systems.

© Armstrong Subero 2021
A. Subero, *Programming Microcontrollers with Python*,
https://doi.org/10.1007/978-1-4842-7058-5_3

These systems in turn consist of two major subsystems which are a hardware component consisting of main processing device and associated electronics and a software system that runs on the hardware configuration.

Embedded systems are sometimes expected to perform their functions in harsh and rugged environments where other computing systems will fail, such as in deep space or under the sea. Some embedded systems are expected to run for years on a single cell, and thus power-efficient design is essential to most embedded systems.

Most embedded systems are designed for real-time operation, meaning the latency of the system must be minimal. In some cases, this latency can cause injury or death if it is not within the required specifications.

Microcontroller vs. Application Processor

Before we go further in our discussion of embedded systems, I think there is an important distinction that must be made. The distinction between the types of processing devices you will encounter in an embedded design. You will encounter systems based around microcontrollers and other systems based around application processors.

A microcontroller (MCU) is a self-contained device that has a processor, memory, and supporting devices integrated into one package. Microcontrollers are usually used in real-time applications or applications where a high volume, low cost, low power, or all three are required.

The birth of the smartphone industry gave rise to the application processor. The application processor can be thought of as a "processor on steroids" as these devices are usually packaged with many CPU cores, graphics processing units (GPUs), cache, multimedia codecs, communication controllers, and a host of other goodies on a single package.

The main difference between the two lies in their intended applications. While microcontrollers are meant for deeply embedded applications with the most complex applications requiring a real-time operating system (RTOS), an application processor will usually have a RTOS at minimum and more commonly will run a general-purpose operating system such as Linux. Application processors may also be used in general-purpose computing systems such as a tablet or smartphone.

Embedded Systems Structure

Despite the changing structure of embedded systems, the majority of systems still utilize the classical structure in their design. The classical structure of an embedded system, as shown in Figure 3-1, consists of four major components. One of the major hardware components of an embedded system is a microcontroller cooperating with a software program which is typically called firmware. The firmware is a software program that is not meant to be changed by the end user. There are also some types of input and output devices communicating with this microcontroller-firmware duo. While this type of configuration isn't going anywhere soon, it is important to acknowledge it is not the only way a system may be structured.

The trend now as shown in Figure 3-2 though is to have a general-purpose application processor system running a Linux-based operating system coupled with a microcontroller device to perform the real-time processing functions. This can be combined in one system in package (SiP) which has all the chips contained in one package or on a board where the application processor may be a system on module which resides close to the "real-time" processor which usually runs a real-time operating system (RTOS) or a bare metal cyclic execution system.

Keep in mind that these are not the only structures of embedded systems as sometimes a programmable logic fabric may exist somewhere in the system. Regardless of how the system is structured, it will receive some input from the input/output (I/O) ports of the system, perform some processing, and then give some useful output to the user via some output device.

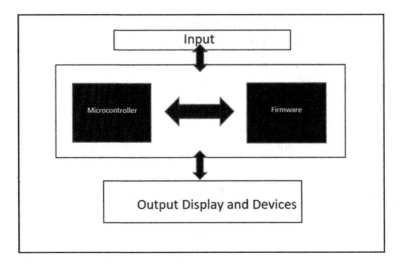

Figure 3-1. *The Classical Structure of an Embedded System*

A typical example of an embedded system with the classical structure would be a calculator. The calculator would receive input via the keypad, then the embedded processor would perform the calculations, and the output would be put onto the screen. Similarly, most "dumb" consumer appliances, office automation equipment, and even subsystems of vehicles all follow this "classic" structure. This is the structure that is the focus of this book as it is the "base" from which other structures are built.

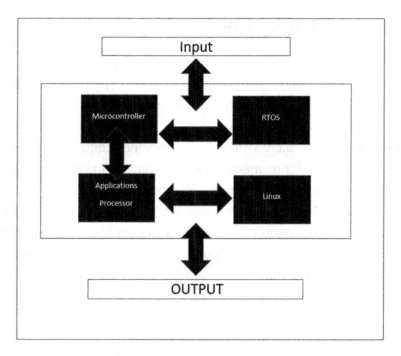

Figure 3-2. *The Trending Structure of an Embedded System*

The "newer" structure once reserved for extremely high-end systems is starting to show up more frequently. The declining cost of silicon with increased computing power combined with a market need for "smart" devices has led to this coupling of applications and real-time processor structure. A robot is the best example of an embedded system that utilizes this structure. You have a microcontroller performing real-time processing that controls the motors and reads sensors and then communicates with the application processor running Linux which uses that data to perform localization and mapping and control the speed at which the platform is moving by communicating with the microcontroller over some serial protocol.

Smart appliances also have this structure, using the application processor running Linux for a rich user experience, which communicates with the underlying microcontroller or several microcontrollers which operate the real-time subsystems.

The Hardware System

As we discussed previously, the components of embedded systems consist of hardware and software working together to perform some task. Regardless of the manufacturer, the hardware will surely consist of a processor, memory, and I/O ports.

The processor is usually a microcontroller which contains a central processing unit (CPU) core, memory, and I/O pins in one package. The common microcontroller cores in use today are ARM, PIC, and AVR architecture. RISC-V is another CPU core architecture that may one day be popular due to the open source nature of the design. Many manufacturers such as Microchip Technology, the maker of the SAM microcontrollers used in many of the CircuitPython boards, will also include peripherals in the package to simplify development time.

The memory included on this package will be divided into two categories which are program memory and data memory. Program memory is usually a flash or FRAM-based nonvolatile storage system and typically ranges from a few kilobytes in size up to a few megabytes. Program memory is used to store the program that will be executed by the CPU core. Data memory on the other hand is memory that is used to store data that is used by the microcontroller during runtime and is typically a few tens or hundreds of kilobytes of SRAM.

I/O pins are the third piece of the puzzle. They allow the CPU core to communicate with devices external to the system such as sensors and other integrated circuits. The amount of I/O a system requires will vary on the application.

Finally, there are peripherals that are included on the hardware device as well. These peripherals may perform a variety of functions such as system support, communications, data conversion, security functions, or debugging and diagnostic capabilities. Some of the newer microcontrollers also have core independent peripherals (CIPs) that perform functions without CPU intervention. Some peripherals such as the direct memory access (DMA) may require initial CPU intervention but then will perform the rest of their functions without further intervention of the CPU.

External to the main processor, the hardware system may consist of other devices such as sensors, user interface devices, or some type of programmable logic device. These all work together to form the hardware component of embedded systems.

The Software System

The software is responsible for making the hardware be useful. The software that runs on an embedded system is called firmware because it is not designed to be changed by the user of the system. This is not set in stone however as updates and upgrades may take place after deployment. This is especially true of modern IoT devices and in a world where consumers expect the "latest and greatest." The general understanding though is that firmware is not meant to be changed.

The software in embedded systems usually falls into two categories. You can either design a bare metal cyclic executive system or you can have a real-time operating system running the system. The difference between the two is the way in which they handle tasks. A task can be thought of as the smallest unit of your firmware program.

In a cyclic executive system, there is only one task that takes the form of what is known as an infinite loop. In such a system, the program would have one main entry point and then cycle through a list of actions that the system must perform. Most embedded designs utilize this type of system. It is simple to implement, and it is used when you don't require much of your system. This is the type of system we will use in the early part of the book.

In an RTOS-based system, there are many tasks that need to be performed. Since the hardware system has limited resources, a scheduler is required to manage the way the tasks access resources. A kernel manages how each task can utilize the hardware resources of the system based on their priority. RTOSs are usually considered an advanced topic and as such will be covered in the advanced portion of the book.

A major facet of firmware development is that it must be designed to be modular. Having modular software is important because it allows you to leverage your existing code base and knowledge across multiple members within a processor family or even across multiple architectures. The ability to use code across platforms is known as portability. Essentially, modularity and portability work in tandem, which we can see in Figure 3-3.

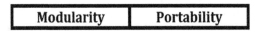

Figure 3-3. *Modularity and Portability Work Together in Good Software Design*

This is important as the skills and time required for new system development can be significantly reduced after an initial investment in the right software development procedures. Sometimes, due to costing or design requirements, you may need to upgrade or downgrade the processor of your design, and you will be thankful that you designed your software to be portable.

The Toolchain

An important part to consider when you are developing embedded systems is the toolchain. The toolchain refers to the tools used for the creation of an embedded system, which include the compiler and programmer/debugger.

Let's first talk about the compiler. The embedded device that we are writing the software on is called the host, usually a PC, MAC, or Linux machine, and the device we are writing the device for is called the target.

The compiler in the embedded toolchain is known in the industry as a cross-compiler. A cross-compiler is a special compiler that runs on the host but with the help of a linker creates a final executable program that is intended for the target.

The second part of an embedded toolchain is the mechanism by which the program created by the cross-compiler is loaded onto the device. Loading is the process whereby a device known as a programmer puts the executable image into the nonvolatile memory of the target. This is usually accomplished via a USB or network link connection between the host and target via the programmer. Many programmers also have debugging capabilities which allow you to verify that a program is working properly. For that reason, many programmers are referred to as In-Circuit Debuggers (ICDs) which allow you to debug the device without removing it from the circuit.

The Joint Test Action Group (JTAG) is an industry standard that is popular for debugging and testing embedded hardware.

The nice thing about a development environment like CircuitPython is that by putting the interpreter on the chip, we can eliminate most of the regular nuances associated with using a traditional development environment. Thanks to the integration of a bootloader, we just have to drop our program onto the chip, and the device will interpret it for us.

Software Testing

A part of embedded software that is usually overlooked is testing. Testing ensures that the embedded software operates as expected; these tests are called functional tests. There is also performance testing which essentially determines if the software meets the "SSS" requirement (speed, stability, and scalability). Performance testing is essentially quality testing. Fault seeding is another common test we can perform in which we introduce faults into the system and determine how it responds. We do this to ensure our exception handling code works correctly.

To aid with testing, many vendors provide a simulator which is a way to ensure your program works properly before you deploy it to actual hardware. Due to the limitations of embedded hardware, sometimes an LED may be the best tool in aiding with testing as it provides visual feedback that the program is working as expected.

Embedded Software Architecture

To keep firmware portable, it is the trend of developers to use what is known as a layered architecture for their firmware ecosystem. What the layered architecture does is separate the specific driver details of how to control the actual hardware from the application itself. Even manufacturers impose this type of design upon developers with all microcontroller vendors providing some sort of hardware abstraction layer (HAL) which uses the principles of reusable firmware by layered architecture in software design.

The type of layered application you will use will depend upon the complexity of your design. The typical layered software configurations you will encounter will usually have from two to seven layers which we will go over now.

The layers may not even have the layout exactly as depicted here, as once they are combined into frameworks (more on this later), it may not exactly look like this rigid layered approach. Some manufacturers lay out their framework that has several layers on the same tier of the framework. Nevertheless, the information I present here will clarify how embedded software is structured. Let us go over the layers one at a time.

The Driver Layer

The driver layer has code that is specific to the CPU core and is the only part of the software architecture that is generally not reusable. This is because even within families of devices, there may be special caveats of peripherals that are specific to that device. Sometimes, silicon bugs exist, and workarounds are necessary to ensure that the developer can still use a peripheral for which the driver is written.

Good drivers have four primary functions. They perform initialization of a peripheral, they configure the peripheral, they perform runtime control, and they properly shut down the driver.

Sometimes, for simple systems, the application layer is built on top of the driver layer. As such, after this point, other layers may not be required, and once the driver layer is in place, the application layer can be on top of any other layer.

What this means is that all subsequent layers can be placed on top of the driver layer but below the application layer. Thus, in my perspective, the driver layer is the most important layer within your software architecture. Many problems that arise later in development can be traced back to this layer. It is crucial that this layer be built as robust as possible.

In case you were wondering what the application layer is, the application layer is the program that contains the tasks you want your system to perform. This is where you implement your program based on your system requirements. We see this structure in Figure 3-4.

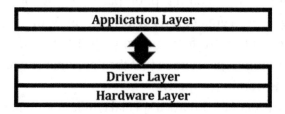

Figure 3-4. *The Driver Layer Is Built on Top of the Hardware Layer*

Hardware Abstraction Layer (HAL)

The next layer is the hardware abstraction layer (HAL). The HAL is placed between the driver layer and application layer.

The HAL adds modularity to the driver layer, allowing the developer to use specific hardware features without any knowledge of the specifics of the hardware. This provides consistency that can be used across device families or even independent of the CPU core architecture. Many microcontroller vendors now provide a HAL that can be used to increase developer productivity. Device manufacturers usually put a lot of resources into providing a good HAL as it allows developers to be able to use their devices as easily as possible.

Figure 3-5 allows us to eliminate the structure.

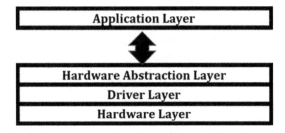

Figure 3-5. *Placement of Hardware Abstraction Layer (HAL)*

Board Support Package (BSP)

Some architectures have a board support package (BSP) on top of the HAL, providing an even greater level of abstraction. Manufacturers usually provide development boards for their products. The manufacturer will provide a board support package so that the developer can test and ensure that everything is working properly.

Due to the layout of the board, a special configuration of software may be needed to ensure proper operation of the board. Sometimes, when you contract a design house to help with product development, they may also provide a BSP especially when the board is expected to run an OS to ensure everything works smoothly. A BSP is good when you plan on iterating upon a design for future boards. This is shown in Figure 3-6.

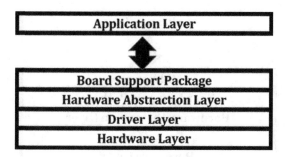

Figure 3-6. *Placement of the Board Support Package (BSP)*

If you are developing a Linux-based system, then the board support package is essential. The BSP will configure the communication buses, clocks, and memory and any other associated peripherals that the operating system needs to work properly. The BSP also usually includes a bootloader which is a small program that runs before the application code runs.

Middleware

One layer that can make your life a whole lot easier and the layer which is usually the topmost layer before the application implementation is the middleware layer. Middleware usually sits between your HAL (or BSP if that layer is present) and application. Middleware connects software components of the board support package with the application layer. Keep in mind that the BSP is optional, so many times what you will find is that middleware connects the HAL directly with the application layer.

Middleware is important because it usually contains software for advanced peripherals and complex protocols. Good vendors provide middleware to ensure their customers use their products. Whereas writing a device driver may take a few hours to some days, the development of middleware is on the scale of a few weeks to months of development time. We see the new structure in Figure 3-7.

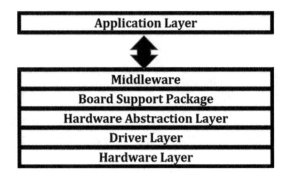

Figure 3-7. *Middleware Placement*

Software Framework

While the layered architecture is good for having a general understanding of how the software is structured, embedded software architecture may be configured in different ways. The specific configuration and layout of the interoperability of these layers is known as a software framework. What a framework provides is a specific configuration of the drivers and middleware libraries that simplifies development. We see what this looks like in its entirety in Figure 3-8.

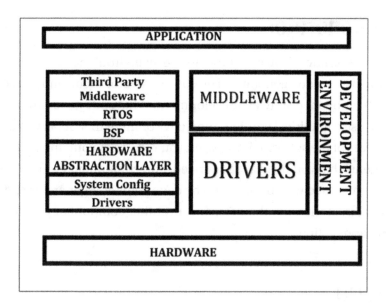

Figure 3-8. *Example Software Framework Mockup*

While the framework mockup in Figure 3-8 does not represent all or any specific implementation, it allows you to understand how a software framework may be structured. A software framework is modular and focuses on being extendable. There is no one way it can be structured and may not necessarily have the rigid layered approach that was presented. Essentially, the framework provides the "scaffold" on which to build your applications. You are usually not expected to modify the framework. However, in practice, you may encounter bugs within a framework which may require modification. Keep in mind that most frameworks have licenses that may restrict changes or require you to publish any changes you have made. It is best to look at the license agreements of the framework you intend to use before you make any modification.

Code Generator

Industry trends have shown that the next level up from the software framework is the code generator. The code generator is currently the final frontier in embedded software development. What code generators do is usually use a graphical configuration environment that details what components of the software framework you require in your application. Components that you need are generated, and components you do not need are not added to your project. The code generator generates code structure, directories, bootloaders, and any other component you need for your end application.

Platform

The combination of hardware and software working together is known as a platform. The platform encompasses the hardware, development tools (including toolchain and IDEs), software framework, and sometimes code generators. A platform can reduce development time significantly. One platform we can use to learn embedded systems is the Arduino platform. The Arduino platform is the entire ecosystem of boards, shields, bootloader, libraries, and development environment. Similarly, CircuitPython follows this concept, combining hardware, software, and development tools. Figure 3-9 shows this relationship.

Figure 3-9. *The Triad Which a Platform Encompasses*

Embedded Systems Constraints

Embedded systems have a variety of constraints in how they are designed. The most common constraints are cost, performance, and energy budget. We will discuss each of these in the following sections.

Cost

Firstly, one of the most critical aspects of embedded systems is their cost. The cost is one of the major driving factors of embedded design. Since most embedded systems are designed into consumer products that will be manufactured in the millions and are essentially "disposable," the cost of the components that go into their design is crucial. Sometimes, a few cents off a design can have a huge impact in the long run.

The list of components used in your embedded design is called a bill of materials (BOM). A term you will come across when discussing cost is the non-recurring engineering (NRE) cost. The NRE cost refers to the initial cost of getting the product into production. Things like research, prototyping, product design, and documentation fall into this category.

Another factor to consider when designing an embedded system is the type of parts you will use. There are commercial off-the-shelf (COTS) parts that are purchased from retailers or directly from manufacturers. There are also application-specific integrated circuits (ASICs) that are designed for a specific purpose you can't find anywhere.

Though some may disagree with me, there is a midway point between a COTS solution and an ASIC, a somewhat hybrid solution of field programmable parts. Devices such as field-programmable gate arrays (FPGAs), programmable logic devices (PLDs), and field-programmable analog arrays (FPAAs) can be purchased "off the shelf" but require the designer to determine what the specific function of the device will be, since they are essentially purchased without a specific function being designed into them.

Sometimes, though, the cost of an embedded design is inescapable. If you are designing for aerospace or deep space applications that require special components, you may not be able to cut costs down. For example, in deep space exploration, radiation-hardened components (rad-hard) can cost several hundred thousand dollars. Here, reliability and quality are more important than cost. In general, you will usually have to make a choice of balance between affordability and quality.

Performance

Performance is a critical aspect of embedded systems design. When we talk about performance, we are talking about the ability of the system to perform its functionality in a reasonable time. The definition of reasonable will be in context of the design. For an electric toothbrush, a reasonable time may be a few seconds, whereas an airbag deployment system will have a few tenths of a second to perform its function. Both hardware and software components may impact the performance of your system.

On the hardware side, processor architecture and clock frequency will have an impact on performance. A 32-bit microcontroller running at 400 MHz will have better performance than an 8-bit one running at 4 MHz. These two go hand in hand, and selecting the right architecture with the right frequency is a skill you will learn with time.

Silicon bugs can also have an impact on performance. In many instances, there will be problems with the CPU core or peripheral that were caused by an error in design by the manufacturer. The result of this error being manufactured into the product results in a silicon bug. These can have a severe effect on performance especially if they are not detected during design. It is necessary to sometimes check the errata sheet of the silicon device you are working with, which can be usually found along with the datasheet.

On the software side, abstraction and algorithm complexity as well as task details can impact performance. Though the current trend in software development is to have a lot of abstraction and implementation of complex algorithms in an application, it is important to remember that the more layers of abstraction you have, the more cycles of CPU time would be required. For this reason, sometimes from the application layer, it may sometimes be necessary to directly call the lower-level driver layer if you need a certain level of performance. Keeping algorithms simple can also greatly reduce development time. In general, remember "KISS" (keep it simple, stupid) when designing your algorithms and software.

Task details refer to how tasks within your system are assigned priorities by the scheduler, and how the tasks communicate with each other can greatly affect performance of your system. According to how your scheduler assigns tasks to your system, it can affect your end application, if there is an error of how resources are allocated. The intercommunication of tasks can also affect performance; if there is information that needs to be passed between tasks, then it must be ensured that there are no errors within the communication between tasks.

Energy Budget

I saved this facet of embedded systems constraints for last as all embedded systems have an energy budget. Even appliances that run off mains electricity have an energy budget as they must be designed with power efficiency in mind. Embedded systems usually run on batteries, and for that reason, they must be as power efficient as possible. The type of power supply you will use will also impact the weight of the device as well as size. I say size because batteries and some power supplies may require special cooling which can add to the overall weight and size of the system.

Developing a battery budget is a good way to ensure that your system is not consuming too much power, though most designers treat power as an afterthought. I will even go so far as to say after you develop your application requirements, before you even select a processor, determine what your battery budget is. Ask the question, how much power will the system use? After you have determined your budget, then you can focus on selecting your processor.

You should also look at the processor power saving modes that are available. This crucial feature can mean the difference between having your product run for days and having it run for months. Read the datasheet of your processor and determine the sleep modes of your processor. Usually, the HAL and driver layer will provide the functions to select a sleep mode type.

Having a dedicated power monitoring circuit, powering external devices from I/O pins, and using modern devices which tend to be more energy efficient are good ways to reduce the amount of power your device will consume.

Embedded Systems Classification

Now that we have a good idea of the hardware and software components of an embedded system and of the restraints, we can focus on understanding how embedded systems are classified. Embedded systems can be classified as small-scale, medium-scale, and high-performance systems.

Small-Scale Systems

Small-scale embedded systems are designed with a single microcontroller, usually an 8-, 16-, or low-feature 32-bit microcontroller. On the hardware side, a single microcontroller controls the entire system. Such systems make up the bulk of embedded systems in our world today. These types of embedded systems usually have the most restraints, usually requiring extremely low cost, low performance, and ultra-low power consumption.

They have a few kilobytes of program memory and a few kilobytes of data memory.

This market is dominated by devices with an 8-bit architecture and may include devices with 4-bit architecture as well (yes, 4-bit). Manufacturers have been trying to design 32-bit devices for this market, and 32-bit is gradually eating 8-bit microcontroller share in this space. Devices in this category are usually required to run for years on a single cell. The "high-end" devices in this category may also have a low-power 16-bit device. Newer ARM-based devices in particular are becoming more capable of meeting these criteria.

On the software side, small-scale systems usually run bare metal with a cyclic executive system and on some occasions may implement a cooperative scheduler. These typically have a two-layer software architecture, and it is possible that assembly code may even be used to develop applications for these devices. These are the types of systems we will focus on in this book as most of your design tasks will be in this category. We see the structure of these systems in Figure 3-10.

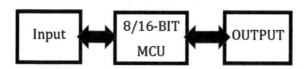

Figure 3-10. *Small-Scale System*

Medium-Scale Systems

Medium-scale embedded systems may have a single processing device or more than one device. They may combine 8-bit microcontrollers and 16-bit or 32-bit processing devices with several hundred kilobytes of data memory and up to about 2 megabytes of program memory. Some vendors also provide 16-bit and 32-bit devices with multiple cores for devices targeted at this category.

The software may consist of a main processor running an RTOS, though the other processors may be bare metal small-scale systems. Assembly language may be used at this level but may be solely on the small-scale subsystems. They may include networking capabilities and are used for "mid-range" embedded design. This type of design is shown in Figure 3-11.

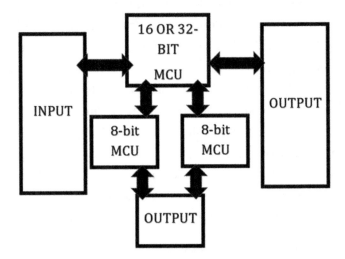

Figure 3-11. *Medium-Scale System*

High-Performance Systems

High-performance embedded systems may have a single processing device or more than one device. They may contain multiple high-end processors and FPGAs, and some may require digital signal processors (DSPs) as part of their hardware design. They may be designed with multiple processor subsystems running RTOSs which themselves consist of several subprocessor systems. Some components may even consist of application processors running a full operating system. These are as expensive and high performance as embedded systems can get.

The software design for such systems usually requires several developers with differing fields of expertise to design. There may also be expensive licensing costs (particularly if using high-end FPGAs) for development tools and debuggers. Additional costs for manufacture and tool vendor support may also need to be purchased.

Distributed Embedded Systems

Medium-scale and high-performance systems may themselves be classified as distributed embedded systems. Distributed embedded systems consist of different subsystems that are each nodes of a larger system. These systems may have different communication models which can be TCP/IP, CAN, LIN, and so on and are the types of systems that exist in wired networks such as those found in cars and airplanes as well as wireless networks such as in the Internet of Things.

Such systems require an experienced architect to design as there will be a need for coordination of system events and design of asynchronous systems is crucial. Fully distributed embedded systems have no "main" processor; all the nodes function independently and are a separate system.

These distributed systems allow for modularity in design which allows separation of safety-critical components from non-safety-critical ones. A safety-critical system is one in which the failure of same will cause serious injury or death to persons or incur substantial financial losses if it should fail. So, for example, in an automobile, having a distributed system will allow separation of the devices controlling the anti-braking system of the vehicle from the infotainment system.

Usually, distributed embedded systems were reserved for large systems such as those in the aerospace, automotive, and military industry. However, what is happening recently is that with the introduction of the Internet of Things which is a type of distributed embedded system, developers need to understand distributed embedded systems.

Seven Steps to Developing an Embedded Product

There are seven steps to developing an embedded product which are idea creation, requirements specifications, functional design, rapid prototyping, testing, securing, and bringing to market.

Step 1: Idea Creation

The first step is probably the most important, that of coming up with your idea. This is arguably the hardest step of the process. The most important thing is that your idea must have an intended target market, and most importantly your product must solve some problem. Many times, the customer will come up with the idea.

Step 2: Requirements Specifications

The second step in your process is to design the requirements specifications. This step is important because you must have a clear direction and focus of what you will be designing. If you have a customer, it is not uncommon that your customer will want a feature and then not want it, leading to disagreements between the customer and the developer. Having a clear requirements specification document will aid as documentary evidence of what the customer wants, or else you may find yourself constantly adding features until you are over budget and behind your time to market. Make sure to include a block diagram in this step showing how the system will be composed.

Step 3: Functional Design

After you have your requirements, the next step is to have a functional design. The requirements specifications describe what we will be designing, and the functional design is how we will go about building it. The functional design will consist of making a model of the system and performing verification. This is the stage where tools such as the Unified Modeling Language (UML) are used to model a system. You should also have functional blocks which further break down the blocks in the requirements section to include more detail.

Step 4: Rapid Prototyping

Traditionally embedded systems development followed several stages or series of steps and used several development processes. These included common software architectures such as Waterfall, V-Cycle, and Spiral-based methods of development. Most books and courses will teach this. However, in the industry, the development trend is toward rapid prototyping. What rapid prototyping does is leverage existing high-level hardware and software tools to implement your product. Rapid prototyping makes use of platforms, code generators, and hardware modules to develop your product. Rather than follow a series of incremental steps, you will generally perform iteration on the design and write software and testing until you have finished design of your prototype.

What this does is give you a prototype at a faster pace and provide a faster time to market (TTM), which refers to the time from coming up with the idea to selling your product. Rapid prototyping saves a lot of time as if you must redesign a prototype; it consists of simply doing a "plug and play" of modules and rewriting software.

Traditionally, you would design a circuit on a breadboard, then spin a PCB board for the prototype, get an enclosure of some type, modify it, and then you would have your prototype. This process was expensive and time-consuming.

With platforms such as the Arduino and technology such as 3D printing, it is possible to get your product very close in look and functionality to the finished design as you can iterate on designs in hours or days instead of weeks or months.

Step 5: Testing

Even though you will be performing testing during the prototyping stage, it is important to perform testing after the product is created. Testing is a complex process that can span several books of information. For this reason, I have included basic tests that you can perform to ensure you have a reasonably functioning system. There is always room for expansion when it relates to testing.

You will perform hardware testing which involves looking for defects and errors in the system. A hardware defect is a difference between the actual prototype and the design. An error occurs when a defective system runs which can lead to failure of the hardware system.

On the software side, it is important to perform software performance testing, with a focus on speed and stability and sometimes scalability. After your prototype is final and you have refactored your software, you must perform unit testing. Unit testing is the process whereby you isolate class and function components of the software and test it in isolation from the rest of the system. You will perform both data testing and scenario testing.

In data testing, you test the isolated function across a wide range of input values. In scenario-based testing, you examine both ordinary use case scenarios where software is in typical use cases and scenarios that are not consistent with ordinary use cases. Such a testing of the system will cause any errors in your system to become visible. Creativity is essential in this type of testing as you will never know what your user will fathom of doing. Try anything and everything you can think about. Test the system in extreme cases. Perform basic tampering and see what happens. You will be glad you did.

You must also perform interaction testing. Interaction testing is a method of testing the interoperability of the hardware and software system. The way you can perform this type of testing is perform fault seeding and see how each component of the system reacts to this fault. Though these testing methods are simple and incomplete, simply performing these tests can put you ahead of the pack of developers that ship products without performing this basic testing. I have seen countless fails of products that would have benefited from just performing these simple steps before the product was brought to market.

Step 6: Securing Your System

Long gone are the days where you did not have to consider security in your system. As software on embedded systems becomes more complex, it is necessary to introduce security measures to protect your embedded system.

Small-scale systems that are not connected to a network generally will require less security measures to be implemented. For such systems, setting some lock bits or fuse bits and enabling code protection may be enough. You can also introduce some type of ID authentication method in software that prevents running of the firmware without the verification. Coating your important components with epoxy is also a good way to secure your system from persons with malicious intent.

While the preceding methods are good for protecting your embedded system that is not connected to a network, there is one addition to your embedded system that poses a huge security risk, that of networking. With the increasing popularity of the Internet of Things (IoT), there has become a need to connect more devices to the Internet. In fact, IoT seeks to connect everything to the Internet.

Some common attacks made against connected embedded systems are broadcast storming, replay attacks, and port probing. A broadcast storming attack is the process of rebroadcasting data through a network link into a node that originally broadcasted the data, causing a failure of the network. A replay attack involves breaking the encryption or using an unsecured network to intercept data communicated on the network and then delaying its transmission or resending it later. Port probing is the process of looking for open ports on a network to exploit vulnerabilities.

Another common way a hacker may exploit the security of embedded systems is using one of the preceding attacks to gain access to your embedded system, reprogramming your device and then using it along with other embedded devices to launch a distributed denial of service attack (DDoS). If you introduced the ID authentication mentioned in the first part of our security discussion, it will prevent the hacker from reprogramming your device and prevent the DDoS attack.

It is impossible to provide all levels of security into your system. The most powerful device is the human mind. Since people are so creative, if a hacker wants to find a way into your system, they will find a way to do so. What you can do is reduce the risk associated with your product by taking the preceding measures. The manufacturer of the SAMD microcontroller commonly used in CitcuitPython based boards, Microchip Technology, also provides solutions to aid with network security and provides use cases for IoT devices. Devices such as the Microchip ATECC608A provide algorithms and security protocols that can be used to secure your device. They provide use cases with two of the largest cloud providers, and it is a good start to adding security to your networked embedded system.

Step 7: Bringing to Market

The final step in creating your embedded device is bringing it to market. This is the longest and most detailed step. In the following steps, you created what is known as an engineering prototype. The steps to bring a device to market are simply too much to cover in this book. As such, if you do not have experience with the process, I recommend you use an engineering firm that focuses on product development.

The reason I recommend you use an engineering firm if you do not have experience is that the industry is a shark eat shark world. Component suppliers and enclosure manufacturers, particularly ones not located in the United States, will steal your design, give you fake components, and may even take your money without providing you the product you paid for. These engineering firms will have connections with verified suppliers and designers and will help you bring your product to market with their expertise.

Conclusion

In this chapter, we looked at all the facets of software development, including an overview of embedded systems, embedded software architecture, classifications of embedded systems, and the steps to developing an embedded product. The information contained in this chapter will serve you throughout your embedded career. The techniques and terminology learned here will aid you as you develop your own microcontroller products using CircuitPython and for when you move up to using complex tools and more high-performance systems.

CHAPTER 4

Python Programming

Python is a large and complex language that I cannot hope to cover in one chapter. There are simply too many functions and structures and programming constructs that need to be detailed to make you into a decent Python user. What I will try to do however is apply the 80/20 rule here, also called the Pareto principle. Since we are learning Python for the purpose of programming microcontrollers with CircuitPython, I can omit a lot of things and still have you understand just enough to follow along with this book.

For that reason, we will learn the 20% of the language that you will need to know to work with 80% of the tasks you are likely to do with CircuitPython. This chapter will thus present a subset of the core language, covering in brief the most important aspects of the language. If you have experience programming with Python, you may think I should have added one or the other. The subset I cover here though is enough so that anyone coming from an Arduino or C background, for instance, will be able to pick up easily.

Writing Python Programs

Python programs are usually written in text files that carry a ".py" extension. Python comes in two versions which are Python 2, the legacy version of Python, and Python 3 which is current and well supported. For most purposes, we will focus on Python 3 since this is the version used in

© Armstrong Subero 2021
A. Subero, *Programming Microcontrollers with Python*,
https://doi.org/10.1007/978-1-4842-7058-5_4

CircuitPython. Should at any point you feel the need to run any programs that are present in this chapter, you can use the Mu editor.

To do this, simply click the mode button as shown in Figure 4-1.

Figure 4-1. *Mode Button*

After you have clicked this button, a window should appear; from the dialog, select the "Python 3" option pictured in Figure 4-2 to start a new Python program.

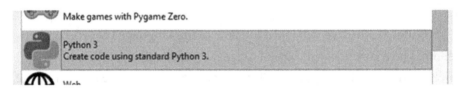

Figure 4-2. *Python 3 Option*

Once it is selected, a window opens; we type our program into the text area and press the run button depicted in Figure 4-3.

Figure 4-3. *The Run Button*

Our program will be run and look for the output in the console window located at the bottom of the IDE. After our program has finished, we can click the stop button as shown in Figure 4-4.

Figure 4-4. *The Stop Button*

Now that you know how to run Python programs, we can look at using the Python language.

It is important to begin our discussion on Python programming by first looking at the typical structure of a Python program. Listing 4-1 shows an example of a basic Python program we will be using through this book. We use the import statement to bring modules in our programs so that we can use methods contained within them. We will also have a main loop called a super loop that runs indefinitely. The words after the hash symbol "#" are called comments. These are ignored by the Python interpreter but allow us to explain to ourselves and other programmers what our code is doing.

Listing 4-1. Basic Python Program

```
# import math modules
import math

# main super loop
while(True):
    # call method from our imported module
    print (math.sqrt(4))
```

In Python, we access methods which are blocks of code that only run when they are called by something called the dot notation. Our math module has a method called square root we would like to use, so we call the "math.sqrt" method. There is also a print statement. The print statement is used to output things to our display that we can use to get information from our program. This basic structure will be maintained for all Python programs, as you will see in later chapters going forward.

Whitespace

Something that should be addressed is that of whitespace in your Python programs. When we talk about whitespace, what we are really talking about are invisible characters such as tabs, blank space, newline characters, and the like.

Whitespace is ignored by some programming languages, but in Python whitespace plays a special role. Whitespace is used to structure your Python programs. While many programming languages use curly braces to indicate where blocks of code start and end, in Python whitespace is used to indicate blocks in the program. Pay attention to whitespace as it is particularly important in your Python code. The programs in this book are fairly short and don't have much levels of indentation; however, you should still pay attention to the whitespace in your programs.

Comments

The comment is the text within your Python program that is there for the benefit of the programmer, as they are ignored by the interpreter. Good programming practice dictates that you include enough comments so that other programmers reading your code will be aware of what the program does. Comments will also remind you what your code did as you may have to update or maintain your code sometime in the future.

Though comments are necessary, it is important not to abuse comments and put too much. As in everything in life, it is important to have balance, so use comments, but don't overuse them.

There are two ways we can write comments in Python. There is the single-line comment that occupies one line and is done by utilizing a hash symbol. Anything put after this symbol is ignored by the interpreter. This is done in Listing 4-2.

Listing 4-2. Single-Line Comment

```
# a single line comment
```

There are also comments that span multiple lines and are used for comment blocks. These use the comment contained within two sets of triple quotes. Listing 4-3 shows us what these multiline comments look like.

Listing 4-3. Multiline Comment

```
"""
a multiline block comment
That spans multiple lines
"""
```

Each comment type has their uses, and it is dependent on the code base you are maintaining or the team you are working with that will determine which comment style you will use.

Variables and Constants

When writing programs, we need some way to store information and retrieve it later. The way we do this is with variables. Variables allow us to assign a name to a memory location, store data at that location, and then retrieve it later. The names we assign to variables in Python must meet certain parameters. Python variables to be valid can be a combination of numbers and characters, also collectively called alphanumeric characters. What this means is that you can only use letters, numbers, and underscores when creating Python programs. Listing 4-4 shows examples of valid Python variable names.

Listing 4-4. Example Valid Python Variable Names

```
Foo
dove
_topshot
RickyTicky99
```

While it is valid to use numbers in a variable name, you cannot begin a variable name with a number. You also cannot have spaces in variable names, and you cannot use keywords (words reserved as part of the language) in variable names. Listing 4-5 shows us some invalid variable names.

Listing 4-5. Example Invalid Python Variable Names

```
20Foo
dove bird
$upermaniac
for
```

To ensure that you do not use any of the reserved keywords as variable names, Table 4-1 shows us which variable names we must not use, sorted in alphabetical order.

Table 4-1. *Reserved Keywords in Python*

and	elif	if	or	yield
as	else	import	pass	
assert	except	in	raise	
break	finally	is	return	
class	False	lambda	true	
continue	for	nonlocal	try	
def	from	None	with	
del	global	not	while	

When variables cannot be changed during program execution, we call these variables constants. In Python, we usually declare variables by writing them in capital letters and placing them in a constants.py file.

Before we can use a variable in a program, we must declare it. Listing 4-6 shows us how to declare a variable.

Listing 4-6. Declaring a Variable

```
# declaring a variable
myVar = None
```

After we declare a variable, we can assign a value to it. The process of assigning a value to a variable is called initialization of the variable. Listing 4-7 demonstrates how we can initialize a variable.

Listing 4-7. Initializing a Variable

```
# initializing a variable
myVar = 10
```

113

As Listing 4-8 shows us, we can both declare and initialize a variable at the same time.

Listing 4-8. Declaring and Initializing a Variable

```
# declaring and initializing a variable
anotherVar = 10
```

Data Types

Variables can belong to one of several data types within the Python language. The type of a variable determines what type of data can be stored within the variable and how much memory it occupies. We don't need to tell Python if a variable is an integer (a number) or a string (like words) as Python automatically handles these assignments. The four data types we use in our programs most often and their use are given in Table 4-2.

Table 4-2. *Common Data Types*

Data Type	Description
int (Int)	This is an integer or a number such as 10, 20, 100, 4000
float (Float)	This is a floating-point number or numbers with a decimal point, for example, 4.5, 60.9, 300.03, 1000.908
str (String)	A string is a set of characters between quotation marks (double or single), for example, "Andy" or 'Maggie'
bool (Boolean)	A data type that can represent True or False

To see the type of your variable, simply use "type(variableName)" and you will see the type of your keyword.

Operators

Python provides facilities to perform many logical and mathematical operations. To accomplish this, Python has a lot of operators it can use. These operators may be arithmetic, relational, logical, bitwise, and assignment operators. Table 4-3 lists some common operators and provides an example of their usage. This table is by no means exhaustive, but it does give you a taste of what is available.

Table 4-3. *Common Python Operators*

Operator	Type	Description	Usage
+	Arithmetic	Adds two operands	X + Y
-	Arithmetic	Subtracts the second operand from the first	X - Y
*	Arithmetic	Multiplies both operands	X * Y
/	Arithmetic	Divides the numerator by the denominator	X / Y
%	Arithmetic	The modulo operator gives the remainder of a division operation	X % Y
**	Arithmetic	This is the exponent operator and performs power calculations	X**Y
==	Comparison	If the two operands are equal, then Python will evaluate the condition as true	A==B
!=	Comparison	If the two operands are not equal, then Python will evaluate the condition as true	A != B
>	Comparison	If the operand on the left is greater than the operand on the right, then the condition is true	A > B
<	Comparison	If the operand on the left is less than the operand on the right, then the condition is true	A < B

Lists

An important component of any programming language is the type of data structures it supports. Lists are one data structure that are fundamental to the Python programming language. Lists store a collection of items that are ordered, and the list can be changed. Listing 4-9 shows us a list in Python.

Listing 4-9. Example List in Python

```
# python list
myList = ["boy", 15, 1.2]
```

Items in a list in Python are assigned an index which starts at 0. We can get the index of a list by using the code in Listing 4-10.

Listing 4-10. Get Index of List Item

```
# get index of list item
myList = ["red", "orange", "green"]
print(thislist[1])
```

Keep this in mind that the elements in a list start at zero as we move forward.

Tuples

A list as we learned in the previous section can store a collection of data types. However, sometimes you need another way to structure your data. For such a scenario, we can use the tuple.

In Python, a tuple structure can be thought of as a list; however, we cannot change the elements contained within the tuple. Listing 4-11 shows us how we use tuples.

Listing 4-11. Python Tuple

```
# tuple example
myTuple=("red", "orange", "green")
print(myTuple)
```

We can access the index of items in a tuple just as we did with a list. Listing 4-12 shows how we can do this.

Listing 4-12. Access Items of Tuple

```
# access tuple item index
myTuple = ("red", "orange", "green")
print(myTuple[0])
```

If Statement

The **if** statement is used to make decisions in your program (see Listing 4-13). To do this, the statement checks a Boolean expression for truth. If the expression is true, the statement will execute.

Listing 4-13. if Statement

```
if (x > y):
    doSomething()
```

else Statement

The **else** statement is used to complement the if statement and create a decision block. The else statement executes when the Boolean statement within the if statement evaluates as false. Listing 4-14 shows us how the else statement would operate.

Listing 4-14. else Statement

```
if (x > y):
   doSomething()

else:
  doSomethingElse()
```

elif Statement

Many times, in our program, we may need to test more than just two conditionals in our decision block. For testing several conditionals, we must use the **elif** statement to test these multiple conditions. Listing 4-15 gives us an example of the else if statement.

Listing 4-15. else if Statement

```
if (x > y):
   doSomething()

elif (x == y):
  doSomethingElse()

else:
   doTheOtherThing()
```

short if

Sometimes, you can put your if statement code on one line if it is short enough and you only have one statement to execute as is shown in Listing 4-16.

Listing 4-16. One-Line if

```
# single line if statement
if x == y: print("its equal")
```

for Loop

Sometimes, we need to execute a block of code for a specified number of times. To aid with this, we use a **for** loop combined with a range function. Listing 4-17 gives an example of a for loop with a range function in action.

Listing 4-17. for Loop

```
# print 0 to 9
for x in range(10):
  print(x)
```

Remember that Python counts from 0, so when the preceding statement is run, it will print numbers from 0 to 9 in the console, not 10.

while Loop

While the for loop with a range function lets us run a block of code for a set number of times, sometimes we are not sure how many times we need to execute a block of code. In such a case, we use a while loop which executes providing the condition specified for the loop's execution remains True this is the basis of many of the programs in this book. Listing 4-18 shows us what the while loop looks like.

Listing 4-18. while Loop

```
while (True):
   runForever()
```

The while loop is used in many embedded applications to keep a program running indefinitely, and when it does so, we call it a super loop.

Functions

Sometimes, within your Python programs, you may find yourself having to run the same block of code over and over. Instead of typing the same block of code multiple times, there is a feature in Python called a function that lets you call a block of code you have written and returns a value. These functions can take arguments on the input and then do something with them. If you need to return a value from a function, you would use the return statement.

For example, let's write a function that will take two variables and raise one to the power of the other and then call it three times to demonstrate how this works as shown in Listing 4-19.

Listing 4-19. Functions

```python
def addVar(a, b):
    print (a**b)

addVar(3, 6)
addVar(2, 8)
addVar(1, 9)
```

Lambda Functions

Sometimes, within our programs, we can create what is known as a lambda function. Lambda functions allow us to write small functions that we don't have to name. Listing 4-20 shows us how we can replace the preceding function with a small lambda function.

Listing 4-20. Lambda Functions

```python
x = lambda a, b : a**b
print (x(2, 5))
```

Exception Handling

Sometimes, parts of our code do not work as intended, and though it may follow all the syntax rules of the program, the statement may still be invalid for execution by the Python interpreter. For example, if we try to print a variable that does not exist, though it is syntactically correct to try to print a variable with the print function, since the variable does not yet exist, we get an error. Instead of crashing the program when we "try" to execute the statement and it fails, we can do something else by placing the block of code under the except statement. Listing 4-21 shows us how exception handling works.

Listing 4-21. Exception Handling

```python
try:
  print(undefVar)
except:
  print("Causes Exception")
```

Object-Oriented Programming

Python is what is known as an object-oriented programming language. What this means is that we can create special bits of code that act as a blueprint by which we can create other code. We call this special blueprint code a class. The formal name for this blueprint is an object constructor, and we use it to create instances of the class. We can also have functions that can exist within a class, and when we do, they are called methods.

Within Python, there exists a special method within the class that is called every time we use it to create an object called the __init__() method. In Python, we can modify instances of the class before it has been called with "self"; using self, we can access attributes and methods of the Python class that will be done to the object once it is initialized.

An object is an instance of the class from which it gets its properties and is meant to model real-world things. Think about a car; two cars may have the same make and model but different colors. They are functionally the same except that the color attribute of them is different. In Python, it is the same way – sometimes, we need objects that are identical but need to modify one a little differently than the other; in such a case, we would create a class, then two instances of that class we can modify separately. Listing 4-22 shows us what a class in Python is like.

Listing 4-22. Python Class

```python
# create the car class
class AwesomeCar:
    # our special method that lets us
    # initialize attributes of the class
    def __init__(self, color):
        # these remain the same
        self.make = "Tayaba"
        self.model = "Nimbus"
        # the colors change
        self.color = color

# create instance of our car class
Car1 = AwesomeCar("Red")

# create another instance of our car class
Car2 = AwesomeCar("Blue")

# print car attributes
# prints {'make': 'Tayaba', 'model': 'Nimbus', 'color': 'Red'}
print(Car1.__dict__)

# print car attributes
# prints {'make': 'Tayaba', 'model': 'Nimbus', 'color': 'Blue'}
print(Car2.__dict__)
```

We can print all the attributes of the class with the (__dict__) which is itself an attribute that objects have which contain all attributes defined for the object itself.

In Python, we will use many classes and their methods throughout this book; this little crash section in objects will be enough to take you through the rest of the book.

Random and Time

Sometimes, we need to generate random numbers, and for that reason, Python provides mechanisms for doing that with a module called the random module. We also have a module called the sleep module that allows our code to wait a certain amount of time. Listing 4-23 demonstrates how we can use these two modules together.

Listing 4-23. Using Random and Time

```
# our random module
import random

# the time module
import time

# super loop
while (True):
    # create a random number between 1 and 10
    x = random.randint(1, 10)

    # print the number
    print(x)

    # once per second
    time.sleep(1)
```

Python vs. CircuitPython

The most widely used distribution of Python is a variety we know as CPython. CPython is the "gold standard" implementation of the Python programming language because it is known as the reference implementation of the language. CircuitPython aims to be compliant with CPython; however, due to obvious reasons of lack of memory on the microcontrollers and for ease of use, some libraries that are available in CPython may not be available in CircuitPython. Most things from the core language do work however, and code written in CircuitPython will be valid in CPython but not necessarily the other way around. The core language however is there, and you can write a lot of amazing programs with CircuitPython.

How Does My Python Program Run?

If you are not familiar with microcontrollers and programming, you may be wondering how a Python program goes from your editor such as Mu into the microcontroller to be executed. So, in this section, I give a high-level overview of what happens when you run your Python program.

Python is what is known as an interpreted language, so what this means is that it takes each statement that is present in our source code and converts it into machine language our microcontroller can understand when the program is run. This is contrasted with a compiler that transforms code written into machine code before the program is run.

Python programs are run in three states which are

- Initialization
- Compilation
- Execution

Before we begin looking at how our Python program is run, we must remember that the Python interpreter is written in C, and as such it is merely a program that is run in our C code. In the initial stage, when we write our program and load it into the C program, the program looks for the Py_main program which is the main high-level function within the main program. Other supporting functions that handle program initialization and the like are then called.

After this stage, we enter the compilation stage where things known as parse tree generation and abstract syntax tree (AST) generation take place to help generate the bytecode. These bytecode instructions aren't machine code; rather they are independent of the platform we are using. The bytecode is then optimized, and we get the object code we need to run. In CircuitPython, we have the option to make our code into bytecode before the program is run, and such files are given a ".mpy" extension. These files can be imported like regular files and are more compact, leading to more efficient memory usage.

Finally, our program is executed within the Python Virtual Machine (PVM). The virtual machine is a function within the interpreter program that runs these bytecode instructions. It's just one big super loop that reads our bytecode instructions one by one and executes them.

Conclusion

In this chapter, we briefly looked at Python and some of the features of the language. Once you read this chapter, you should have a basic understanding of the Python programming language. Programming is something though that you learn over time, and as such it is important that we write code. Only by writing code will you learn the language you are using, and for that reason, in the next chapter, we will look at how we can use Python to control our microcontroller hardware.

CHAPTER 5

Digital Control

At this point, we have covered enough about electronics, embedded systems architecture, and programming to begin using physical microcontroller devices. Now we will learn the basics of undoubtedly the most important operations you will handle with your microcontroller: input and output. At the heart of every microcontroller system, you will at a minimum have an output being performed, and many systems take in inputs as well.

In this chapter, you will begin to see how to control and manipulate physical sensors and actuators. There is something satisfying about manipulating physical I/O devices that just cannot be matched by pushing pixels around a screen. I hope this chapter will introduce you to the joys of working with hardware and whet your appetite for further experiments with microcontroller development.

I/O Pins

Microcontroller devices have physical pins attached to them. These pins have a valuable purpose: they allow the microcontroller device to be interfaced to the outside world. As we've discussed previously, a microcontroller system typically takes an input of some sort, performs some processing, and then provides an output that manipulates some external peripheral or device. This is the premise of input and output control.

© Armstrong Subero 2021
A. Subero, *Programming Microcontrollers with Python*,
https://doi.org/10.1007/978-1-4842-7058-5_5

Generally, you can tell a lot about a microcontroller from the number of input and output pins it controls. More pins on a microcontroller means the device will usually contain more peripherals and have a powerful CPU core. Microcontrollers typically have at least six I/O pins. Sometimes, they can have hundreds.

In the past, it was common for a microcontroller to come in a DIP package. You would need to connect it to a programmer and set up the proper connections and power configurations before you could use it. While this may be good in a professional setting, it is overly complicated for makers and people just getting started with microcontrollers. The rise of the development board has simplified the process for hobbyists. The board comes with a microcontroller in a known working state, allowing the user to concentrate right away on building circuits and attaching external devices and also focus on writing software.

Output and Input on Microcontroller Hardware

On the underlying hardware, microcontrollers typically perform output using what is known as a port. In its simplest form, a port can be thought of as a collection of pins that allow the microcontroller to be interfaced to the outside world.

Ports are usually arranged in groups of pins; typically around 8 or 16 pins make up a port, and this can be as high as 32 pins. You may be wondering why we need to group microcontroller pins in the ports in the first place. What you must know is that in the microcontroller architecture, the ports are nothing more than registers. Thus, there is some correlation between the number of pins in a port and the architecture of the microcontroller. So, an 8-bit microcontroller typically has ports that have 8 pins, and 16-bit microcontrollers have ports that have 16 pins. This is not set in stone however; you may have a 32-bit microcontroller, for example, that has ports that are 16 bits wide (have 16 pins) or may even have as low as 4 pins to a port. As a user of microcontroller devices, you can simply think of this as a manufacturer's design decision. You should also know that since a port is a register, each pin on that port is a bit in the register. Ports are given a designation such as PORTA or PORTB, and the pins within each port are numbered. Let's imagine we have a hypothetical microcontroller with two ports, PORTA and PORTB, as shown in Figure 5-1.

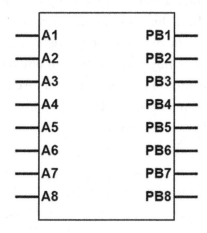

Figure 5-1. *A Hypothetical Microcontroller with Two Ports*

The pins on PORTA are all designated with the names "AX," where "X" is a bit associated with that port. So, for example, the A1 pin refers to the first bit on PORTA. Shortened names like "A1" make for easier identification and labeling, and they also help when you need to access a particular pin when you're writing code for the microcontroller.

The pins on PORTB in Figure 5-1 follow a different naming convention than those on PORTA: "PBX" rather than "BX." Different manufacturers follow different naming conventions for port pins. Some will use the names like "A1" and "D1," while others will use names like "PA1" and "PD1." Only the naming convention changes. The pins themselves work the same way. In practice, it is common for microcontrollers to have their pin numbers start from 0. Thus, the first pin in PORTA is typically called something like A0 or PA0.

For simplicity, it would be nice for each pin on a microcontroller to have a dedicated function. For example, we can imagine that PORTA on our hypothetical device is an output port, which means that the pins on the port can only carry data out of the microcontroller. Similarly, we can imagine that PORTB is an input-only port, being able to only accept data from the outside world and into the microcontroller.

However, what would happen if we had an application where the microcontroller must interface with a lot of output devices, like controlling 15 lights? Or we could have the microcontroller control a keypad that has 12 inputs? In both cases, the number of pins we have available for input or output would be limited if they are only used for one purpose. As such, it is common to have the pins on a microcontroller be configured as input or output based on the discretion of the circuit designer.

To allow for this, there must be some mechanism internal to the microcontroller that will allow pins on the ports to be used as either input or output. Thus, in many microcontrollers, it is common to have a register that can control the direction of data into and out of the pin. This register is programmed via software and is controlled by the microcontroller programmer.

When used in this way where the port can be configured as simply an input or an output, the port pin is said to be in a digital state. When in the digital state, the pins can be configured in several ways; usually, we say that it has three states. As an output, it can be configured as output high, where the pin is an output and is providing current to the load. The pin can also be an output low, where the pin is still configured as an output pin but is not providing current to the load. The pin can also be configured as an input.

Not only is it common to have internal circuitry that can control the direction of the pins, but many times a microcontroller has other internal peripherals and modules that depend on these same pins to perform their input and output function. These include things like serial interfaces, using internal timers or analog functions. These are known as alternate functions of the pin, and these vary depending on the manufacturer.

This is necessary as while most microcontrollers include many features and onboard peripherals, most applications only require one or two of these peripherals to be used at any point in time. Thus, in order to ensure that we don't need pins for every peripheral present on the microcontroller, this internal circuitry will ensure that onboard functions can be shared among limited I/O pins (remember the multiplexer we talked about earlier? This is an application for that device within the microcontroller). For that reason, it is common to see a microcontroller more closely resemble the diagram in Figure 5-2.

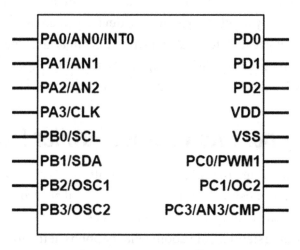

Figure 5-2. *A More Realistic Microcontroller*

The microcontroller in Figure 5-2 represents a more accurate depiction of what a microcontroller will look like when you consider the fact that most pins include alternate functions. As you can see, there are multiple ports: PORTA, PORTB, PORTC, and PORTD. Each of these ports has pins with various functions. The VDD pins and VSS pins on all microcontrollers are not associated with any I/O port as they provide power to the device. An experienced designer will be able to look at a similar diagram and realize which pins are used for which purpose. For example, we know that pin PA0 will most likely be used for both digital input and output. However,

131

the label AN0 is also attached to the pin. This means the pin can also be used for an analog input functionality. The third label, INT0, means that we can use the pin for external interrupt capability as well.

As you gain more experience with design and become more familiar with different microcontroller families, you will be able to look at the ports on the circuit diagram and know which pins have what alternate functionality. Even with such experience, though, you cannot always tell what purpose a pin may serve. For example, look at pin PC3. Thanks to the alternate AN3 label, you may think that it can be used for both digital and analog functionality, but what does the CMP label mean? Such questions are best answered by the datasheet for the device you are working with. The datasheet may reveal, for example, that this pin is an input-only pin and cannot be used for any digital output functionality. Be sure to keep a copy of the device datasheet on hand to answer questions such as this.

Going Deeper into Microcontroller I/O

You may be wondering how exactly a microcontroller is able to perform the input and output using the pins. While the digital electronics behind how this works can get quite complicated, we can look at some basic circuit constructs to understand a little about what happens at the lowest level.

In the case of an output pin, look at the circuit diagram in Figure 5-3.

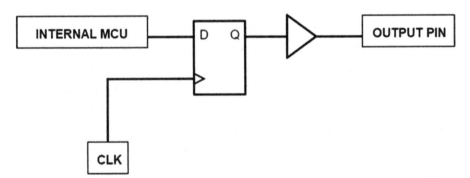

Figure 5-3. *MCU Output Circuit*

In this scenario, we have a flip-flop or some other latch circuit that is under CPU control. Do you remember when we talked about the flip-flop? Well, this is one application of the flip-flop within the microcontroller. Remember we said that the flip-flop can store a single bit of data at a time. Well, when our pin is set as an output, we can output a high value (logical one) or output a low value (logic zero). The flip-flop is used to store the desired bit we want (high or low). The output of the latch circuit passes through a buffer. This buffer circuit allows for a greater drive strength and gives the microcontroller internals better protection from electrical disturbances that may be present external to the device. Also not shown here are protection diodes which work together with the buffer to protect the microcontroller. The output of the buffer circuit then connects to the physical pin on the microcontroller.

Similarly, we can gain an understanding of how input on a microcontroller works by looking at the circuit diagram in Figure 5-4.

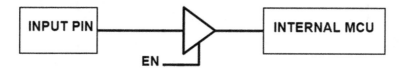

Figure 5-4. *MCU Input Circuit*

In this case, the pin connects to a buffer that has an enable function. When the CPU manipulates the enable pin to the buffer (which of course it will do based on instructions in the program code), the voltage level of the pin can then be read, and the CPU can then use this information for any purpose.

Of course, in real MCUs, the circuit can get more complicated than this because the pins on the microcontroller must act as both input and output. This is called bidirectional control, and it allows the microcontroller to use a single pin for input and output.

Our look at input and output circuits leads us to another consideration when working with microcontroller I/O pins: the ability of a microcontroller port to sink or to source current. Sourcing current refers to a microcontroller's ability to supply current to the load. That is to say, current will flow from the microcontroller pin, through the load, and then to the ground. Figure 5-5 depicts what sourcing current looks like.

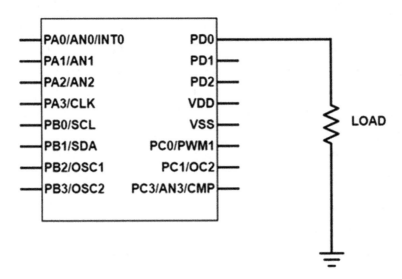

Figure 5-5. *MCU Sourcing Current*

A microcontroller I/O pin can also sink current. In this case, current flows from the supply source, through the load, and into the I/O pin. Figure 5-6 shows what sinking current looks like.

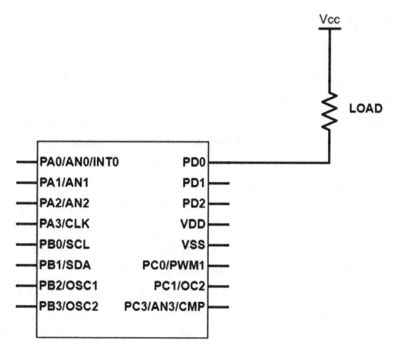

Figure 5-6. MCU Sinking Current

Using Output: Lighting an LED

Now that we understand a little about microcontroller ports, we can look at using output to perform a function: in this case, lighting up an LED. Much like printing "Hello, world!" is a traditional first step when learning a new coding language, operating an LED is a traditional first task when working with a new microcontroller. It allows you to verify that you have a working program and that all your connections are accurate. In this section, we will look at how to build a physical circuit to connect your microcontroller to an LED. Then we will cover how to use CircuitPython to control the microcontroller's output and make the LED light up.

LED Control

Recall from Chapter 2 that LEDs are special diodes that emit light when a current flows through them. To drive an LED, you will need voltage to flow into the LED. Though the microcontroller can supply a regulated voltage into the LED, the current must also be regulated to avoid damaging it, as LEDs have a maximum current rating that you must not exceed. To regulate the current through the LED, you can use a resistor.

There is also a voltage drop associated with using an LED. The typical red LED, for example, will drop approximately 2 volts. Different LED colors drop different voltages, however, and the voltage drop will vary by manufacturer as well. It is best to consult the datasheet for the device you are using to get the exact specifications for your LED.

Knowing the voltage drop, you can calculate the output current that will flow through the LED. If the microcontroller gives a 5-volt output, then with a voltage drop of 2 volts given by the LED, the series resistor will have a voltage of 3 volts across it. If you want a maximum current of 10 mA to flow through the LED (you can find the actual number on your datasheet), then you can use Ohm's law to calculate what resistor is needed.

To use Ohm's law, divide the voltage by the current. This would be 3 V / 0.01 A. This yields 300 ohms, the minimum level of resistance needed to protect the LED. In this case, a 470-ohm resistor is a good choice. Remember, each resistor has a tolerance level that can make the actual resistance less than the expected value, so it would be risky to use the exact resistance value you calculate. If you want close to maximum brightness, then a 330-ohm resistor will suffice.

Building the Circuit

Once you have made your calculations, you are ready to design a circuit that will allow your microcontroller to control an LED. The circuit will look something like the schematic shown in Figure 5-7.

CircuitPython MCU

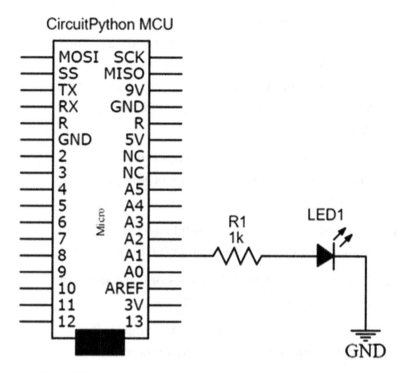

Figure 5-7. *MCU Circuit LED*

We also use a 1k resistor to limit the amount of current that flows from the device; remember you will have no problem using a higher value resistor, and it is desirable if you want greater power efficiency as a higher resistor will draw less current.

You can follow the following steps to set up this simple circuit. Be sure that you connect your circuit before you power up your device.

1. Make sure that your microcontroller is properly powered by connecting the microcontroller to your power supply; if you are using a development board, then your USB connection will be sufficient to power up the device. If you wish to connect your external power supply, then connect the Vout of your power supply to the Vin input of your board

137

(the value of the power supply output voltage is usually from 7.5 to 12; this varies depending on the board you are using, so be sure to consult the user manual of your board to see the input voltage range) and connect the ground to the ground pin of your microcontroller board.

2. Connect a jumper wire from the A1 pin on your microcontroller to a socket on the prototyping area of your breadboard.

3. Connect one lead of the resistor to another socket in the same row of the breadboard used in step 2.

4. Connect the other end of the resistor to a socket in a different row of the breadboard.

5. Connect the long lead of the LED to a different socket in the same row of the breadboard used in step 4.

6. Connect the short lead of the LED to a socket in a different row of the breadboard.

7. Connect a jumper wire to a different socket in the same row of the breadboard used in step 6.

8. Connect the other end of the jumper wire to the ground.

When you have finished connecting the circuit, it should look similar to Figure 5-8.

Figure 5-8. *MCU LED Circuit on a Breadboard*

Lighting an LED with CircuitPython

Now that we've covered building the physical LED circuit, we can look at how to control the LED using CircuitPython. The program we will write will turn the LED on. Open the Mu editor and type the program into your "code.py" file as shown in Listing 5-1.

Listing 5-1. Controlling the LED

```
# import pin constants for board we are using
1 import board

# import pin control
2 import digitalio

# create object for pin we are using
3 led = digitalio.DigitalInOut(board.A1)

# set the pin to output
4 led.direction = digitalio.Direction.OUTPUT

# turn the LED on
5 while True:
    led.value = True
```

The first thing we do in this code is import the CircuitPython libraries needed to control the board. CircuitPython provides many libraries to perform digital I/O. At **1**, we import the board module, which contains the pin constants for the board being used. With this module imported, we can refer to pins by their names – for example, A1. At **2**, we import the digitalio module. It contains all the classes that provide access to the input and output function we'll be using. Among other things, the module lets us set the pin direction to determine if we are reading data into a pin or writing data out of it.

With the necessary libraries imported, at **3** we create an instance of the pin object we are using. This instance has its own place in memory, and doing this allows us to access all the methods that are present within the "digitalio" module that we imported. This is vanilla Python syntax and shows us that our regular Python abilities can be utilized within CircuitPython programs. We then use that instance to set the direction of the LED at **4**. In this case, we set the direction to output.

At this point, everything is set up, so we can now turn the LED on. At **5**, we create what in the world of embedded systems is commonly called a super loop. Any instructions that fall within a while True statement will be performed over and over again, until the program is told to stop. In this case, we set the value of the led object to True, meaning the LED will light up.

We use a super loop because there is no operating system to do any control for us. The while True line ensures we keep performing our LED on action over and over. If you omit this line, then the LED will be lit once for a short period of time (too short for us to see). Almost all programs you will write for your microcontroller will contain such a super loop.

Hit the **Save** button in the Mu editor; this should save the changes to your "code.py" file, and you will observe that the LED connected to pin A1 has been lit. Now that you have successfully controlled digital output, feel free to experiment a little bit. Can you make the LED be controlled by pin A0? Or pin A2? To do this, you would simply rewire your circuit to the different pin and change the pin number when we are creating the pin object.

If your circuit is not working, make sure and test your connections; by that I mean make sure your wires are properly pushed into the holes designated for them. Check, check, and check again.

Blinking an LED

Turning on an LED is fun and all, but it is a bit boring. If we connected the LED directly to the power supply using a resistor, we would have the same effect. The beauty of intelligent control is that we can do things intelligently.

For example, you can program your microcontroller to not only turn on the LED but also to turn on the LED at time intervals of your choosing. This program will let you verify that your clock is set up properly, as you can look at the rate at which the LED is flashing. If the LED flashes at an incorrect rate, you will need to ensure you have the proper board selected or may need to check your USB and circuit connections. You've already set up the physical circuit. All you need to do is update your code with a few more lines. You can use the program given in Listing 5-2.

Listing 5-2. Blinking the LED

```
# import pin constants for board we are using
import board

# import pin control
import digitalio

1 # import time library
import time

# create object for pin we are using
led = digitalio.DigitalInOut(board.A1)

# set the pin to output
led.direction = digitalio.Direction.OUTPUT
```

```
# super loop
while True:
    # turn the LED on
 2 led.value = True

    # sleep for a second
 3 time.sleep(1)

    # turn the LED off
 4 led.value = False

    # sleep for a second
 5 time.sleep(1)
```

In this program, in addition to importing the board and digitalio modules, as we did in Listing 5-1, we also import the time library at **1**. This library contains functions that will allow the microcontroller to follow time-related instructions. In particular, we'll use the time library's sleep method. It tells the microcontroller to wait for a certain amount of time, specified in seconds.

After initiating the led pin object as we did in Listing 5-1, we enter a super loop with a while True statement, as before. This time, the loop contains a few more instructions. At **2**, we turn the LED on, just like in Listing 5-1. At **3**, we tell the microcontroller to wait by passing a value of 1 second in the sleep method. At **4**, we turn the LED off by setting the value of the led object to False. Then we use sleep again at **5** to delay for another second before restarting the loop.

Hit the "Save" button in the Mu editor, and you will observe that the LED connected to pin A1 flashes on and off every second. If you wanted to make the LED blink faster, you could pass a smaller value, like 0.5 seconds, into the sleep method. If you wanted the LED to run slower, you could use a longer value like 2 seconds instead.

Using Input: Adding a Pushbutton

The next time we work with our board, we will be looking at digital input. To do this, we will be adding a pushbutton to the circuit. Input is the complement to output on the microcontroller, and together they make up the two most basic microcontroller operations. If using an LED is like the "Hello World" of embedded development allowing you to print something to your screen, then reading a pushbutton will be equivalent to learning to read input from your keyboard. Our input project will be reading the state of a pushbutton on one pin, and then depending on the state read, we will toggle an LED connected to another I/O pin.

Pull-Up vs. Pull-Down Resistors

Before we start building the circuit, it's important to note that there are different ways to connect a pushbutton to a microcontroller pin. You can do so using either a pull-up or a pull-down circuit configuration. The schematic for a pull-up configuration is shown in Figure 5-9.

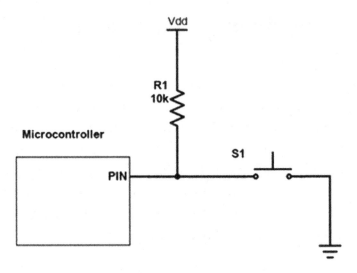

Figure 5-9. *Pull-Up Configuration*

In pull-up configuration, we use a resistor with a high value (usually between 4.7 and 10k) to pull up (which is to say, connect the I/O pin to VDD via the resistor) one side of the pushbutton to VDD. This resistor ensures that when the pushbutton is pressed, little current will flow from the circuit.

Figure 5-10 shows a schematic for a pushbutton in pull-down configuration.

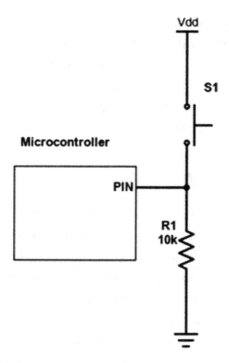

Figure 5-10. Pull-Down Configuration

Whereas the pull-up resistors pull the pin up to a high value, a pull-down resistor pulls the pin down to a logical low value, which is to say we connect the I/O pin to the ground through the resistor. To connect a switch in pull-down configuration, the switch must be placed between the supply voltage and the microcontroller pin.

When you use a pull-up configuration, the circuit will be active low, while with a pull-down configuration, the circuit will be active high. Generally, you will use your pushbuttons with pull-up resistors, and most microcontrollers provide pull-up resistors on their pins. Either configuration will work, however. Depending on your circuit application, one or the other approach might be preferable.

Later in this section, we will look at how to use the microcontroller with both a pull-up and pull-down circuit configuration. For other circuits in this book, though, I will only use the pull-up configuration. If you wish, you can modify any circuit in this book to use the pull-down configuration without having any adverse effect on circuit operation by following the pull-down model demonstrated as follows.

Switch Debouncing

Another facet to consider when working with microcontroller inputs once we are using a type of switch is switch debouncing. No device is perfect, and the more moving parts a device has, the more problems there will be associated with it. This is also true of mechanical pushbutton switches when they must be interfaced to microcontroller circuits.

Due to their construction, when you press a pushbutton switch, the microcontroller may register multiple presses of the switch. This effect is similar to what happens when you drop a ball. The ball does not immediately come to rest, but instead bounces for a few intervals of time. Likewise, when you push a switch, it does not have one solid close. There are a series of openings and closings that take place when the switch is closed.

Because of this bouncing effect, there's a risk that the microcontroller will register the switch as open when it's meant to be closed. To counteract this problem, you can implement a technique called switch debouncing. This can be done using either hardware or software.

For hardware debouncing, we can use a flip-flop (latch), as is shown in Figure 5-11. The flip-flop works as a switch debouncing as once Q is set to a high state by the input, there are no further changes that will occur at the output of Q. The flip-flop will latch the value of the input whenever there is a change in state. There are other methods of hardware debouncing such as using a Schmitt trigger; however, the flip-flop method is simple and effective.

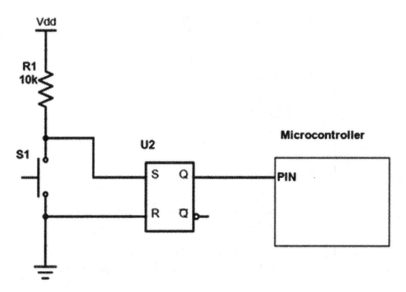

Figure 5-11. *Flip-Flop Debounce*

Instead of adding a piece of hardware, you can also build a debouncing effect into your code. There are several software debouncing methods, including using counters and software shift registers. Later in this section, we will use a simple software delay to debounce the pushbutton switch.

Input with MCU Schematic (Pull-Up)

We can build a simple pushbutton circuit by building the program that is shown in Figure 5-12. In this circuit, we use the switch in pull-up configuration.

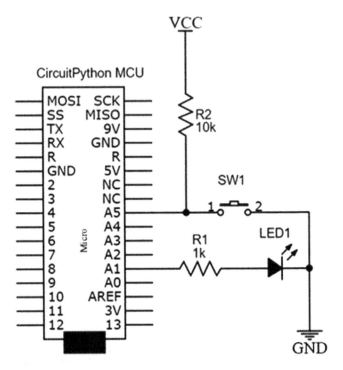

Figure 5-12. *MCU with Pull-Up Switch*

Pushbutton Pull-Up Circuit Connection Tips

This circuit is simple and hard to mess up. If your circuit is not working, make sure and test your connections. Check, check, and check again. Ensure that you connect your circuit before you power up your device.

These are the recommended steps to connect the circuit:

1.   Connect the LED as we did in the previous section as per schematic diagram. To make it easier, you may want to run one jumper wire from the 3.3v voltage output socket on your development board to the positive rail and the other jumper wire from the ground connection to the ground rail. To make

layout easier, and better utilize the board, you can connect both positive rails together and both negative rails as well.

2. Place the switch across the ravine in the center of the board, ensuring both pins on either side of the switch are placed into sockets of the prototyping area of your breadboard.

3. Connect one end of the switch to one end of the resistor in the same socket and the other end of the resistor to the positive rail. There is no need to use a jumper wire as the resistor can directly be connected to the LED.

4. Connect the other end of the switch to the ground using a jumper wire.

5. Run a jumper wire from the intersection point between the switch and resistor that leads to PIN A5 on your MCU. To accomplish this, ensure that the lead of the switch, the lead of the resistor, and the jumper wire are all in the same sockets.

When you have finished connecting the circuit, it should look like Figure 5-13.

Figure 5-13. *MCU Pull-Up Circuit on a Breadboard*

Pushbutton Pull-Up with CircuitPython Program

Once we have our circuit connected, we can write a program that will allow the MCU to use the pushbutton in a pull-up circuit configuration. Edit the code.py file so that it resembles Listing 5-3.

Listing 5-3. Reading a Pushbutton with MCU Pull-Up

```
# import pin constants for board we are using
import board

# import pin control
import digitalio

# import time library
import time

# create object for LED we are using
1 led = digitalio.DigitalInOut(board.A1)
```

```
# create object for the switch we are using
            switch = digitalio.DigitalInOut(board.A5)

# set the LED to output
led.direction = digitalio.Direction.OUTPUT

# set the switch to input
            switch.direction = digitalio.Direction.INPUT

# super loop
2 while True:
        # if our pin goes low
          if switch.value == False:
        # wait 100 ms to see if switch is still on
                3 time.sleep(0.1)

      # if the switch is still on
        4 if switch.value == False:
            # turn the LED on 5
            led.value = True

    else:
        # turn the LED off 6
        led.value = False
```

Save the file and observe what happens. When you press the pushbutton, the LED will light up, and when you release it, the LED will stop being lit.

Do you understand what is happening here? Let us go through the program. We do our usual imports and set up objects for the LED and switch we are using at **1**. Once we have these set, we set the direction of the LED to output and the direction of the switch to be an input after **1**. Our super loop is where it all happens.

Within our super loop at **2**, we use a conditional if/else statement to test our program to see if the pushbutton is pressed. If the pushbutton is pressed, then we wait 100 milliseconds at **3**. If after the 100 milliseconds has passed, the pushbutton is still pressed at **4**, then we turn the LED on at **5**. To accomplish this task, we use a nested if statement. This checking the pushbutton, waiting, then checking the pushbutton again is the switch debouncing we were talking about. At **6**, we turn the LED off which is the default state of the program.

When we look at the conditional, we see that if the pushbutton is low, then we turn the LED on. If this is confusing to you, remember that the pull-up resistor will set the pin to a default high state, so our MCU will be reading a high state on the pin constantly. Essentially, since we have a pull-up resistor connected to the pin, then the pin will be held high up to VCC which is 3.3 volts. When we press the pushbutton, the pin will be pulled low to the ground. We can also use the pushbutton in a pull-down state as we will learn in the next section.

Input with MCU Schematic (Pull-Down)

We can build a simple pushbutton circuit by building the program that is shown in Figure 5-14. In this circuit, we use the switch in pull-down configuration.

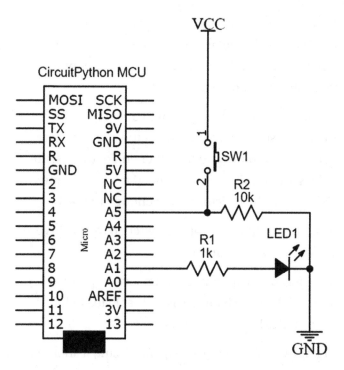

Figure 5-14. MCU with Pull-Down Switch

Pushbutton Pull-Down Circuit Connection Tips

If your circuit is not working, make sure and test your connections. Check, check, and check again. Ensure that you connect your circuit before you power up your device.

These are the recommended steps to connect the circuit:

1. Connect the LED as we did in the previous section. To make it easier, you may want to run one jumper wire from the 3.3v voltage output socket on your development board to the positive rail and the other jumper wire from the ground connection to the ground rail. To make layout easier, and better utilize the board, you can connect both positive rails together and both negative rails as well.

2. Place the switch across the ravine in the center of the board, ensuring both pins on either side of the switch are placed into sockets of the prototyping area of your breadboard.

3. Connect one end of the switch to one end of the resistor, ensuring that they are in the same socket on the breadboard, and the other end of the resistor to the ground rail; there is no need to use a jumper wire here as the resistor is long enough to reach.

4. Connect the other end of the switch to the positive supply rail using a jumper wire.

5. Run a jumper wire from the intersection point between the switch and resistor that leads to PIN A5 on your MCU.

When you have finished connecting the circuit, it should look like Figure 5-15.

Figure 5-15. *MCU Pull-Down Circuit on a Breadboard*

Pushbutton Pull-Down with CircuitPython Program

Once we have our circuit connected, we can write a program that will allow the MCU to use the pushbutton in a pull-up circuit configuration. Once you have built your circuit you can connect your board and edit the code.py file so that it resembles Listing 5-4.

Listing 5-4. Reading a Pushbutton with MCU Pull-Down

```
# import pin constants for board we are using
import board

# import pin control
import digitalio

# import time library
import time

# create object for LED we are using
led = digitalio.DigitalInOut(board.A1)
```

```
# create object for the switch we are using
switch = digitalio.DigitalInOut(board.A5)

# set the LED to output
led.direction = digitalio.Direction.OUTPUT

# set the switch to input
switch.direction = digitalio.Direction.INPUT

# super loop
while True:
    # if our pin goes high
  1 if switch.value == True:
        # wait 100 ms to see if switch is still on
  2     time.sleep(0.1)

        # if the switch is still on
  3if switch.value == True:
            # turn the LED on
            4led.value = True

    else:
        # turn the LED off
        led.value = False
```

Save the file and observe what happens. You will get the same effect as when you used the MCU with the pushbutton connected as a pull-up. When you press the pushbutton, the LED will light up, and when you release it, the LED will stop being lit.

The only change you will see is to the conditional statement that checks the pushbutton. When we look at the conditional at **1**, we see that if the pushbutton is high, we wait for 100 ms at **2**, then at **3** once the switch is still pressed, and then at **4** we turn the LED on. We must remember that since we have a pull-down resistor connected to the pin, then the pin will be held low to the ground. When we press the pushbutton, the pin will get current from the power supply.

You can try using a different pin to connect the pushbutton with. Don't be afraid to experiment and keep trying new things. Remember that is the only way you will learn; try swapping pins, try changing your "True" condition to false, and observe the effect it will have (the LED will be on until you press the button, then it will turn off). That is all you need to do to learn how to use your microcontroller.

Conclusion

In this chapter, we covered a lot of information related to input and output on a microcontroller. We learned about microcontroller ports and how we can use them as input and output. We looked at how we can use output to control LEDs and how we can use input to control pushbuttons, in both pull-up and pull-down states. In the next chapter, we'll expand beyond digital signals and look at how we can perform analog input and output and use this to interface to analog devices as well.

CHAPTER 6

Data Conversion

One of the main strengths of microcontrollers is their ability to digitize the analog information we're so familiar with working with, like temperature, humidity, and light intensity. We can take these analog sensor readings and convert them into digital form as signals that we can analyze and manipulate. Converting analog signals into digital signals is a hallmark for microcontroller devices, as many applications of the smart devices that utilize microcontrollers will monitor sensors and then perform some action based on that data. Analog to digital conversion is an essential topic for anyone interested in microcontrollers.

In this chapter, we look at analog to digital conversion, then look at some sensors we can get data from using this method. The sensors we will use include a potentiometer, a photoresistor, and a temperature sensor.

Analog to Digital Conversion

Any decent microcontroller will be outfitted with analog to digital conversion modules. *Analog to digital conversion* (ADC) modules convert the information presented to them into a binary representation that the microcontroller can manipulate.

Our physical world is analog in nature. Take your phone's recording system: you speak into your phone's microphone, and the signal received is analog. The microphone must then convert this analog information from your voice into a digital signal representation that can be interpreted by

© Armstrong Subero 2021
A. Subero, *Programming Microcontrollers with Python*,
https://doi.org/10.1007/978-1-4842-7058-5_6

your microcontroller. One application of this would be in voice recognition systems where a microcontroller in your device needs to listen for a "wake-up word." A "wake-up word" is a word or phrase you can use to get the attention of your computing device. The microcontroller would need to convert your voice into a digital form so that it can search for the word, which would wake up the device from sleep. Most smartphones also incorporate features that filter out background noise or amplify voice signals. Using the ADC module of a microcontroller, you can easily filter out noise from the audio coming into the microphone. This type of filter though is not like the hardware filters we learned about in Chapter 2 but is in fact a digital one which operates in software. Their function however is similar to the filters you learned about previously.

As we learned in Chapter 2, analog circuits are known as continuous circuits; thus, the signals produced by them are continuous in nature. When we say a signal is continuous, we mean that it is characterized by smooth transitions between points in the signal with a variation in time. A digital signal, being produced by digital circuits, as we learned has a discrete nature. For our purpose, these can be thought of as a digital representation of a continuous signal.

Let's first take a closer look at what's meant by a signal. A signal can be thought of as energy that we can use to extract information. Within the context of microcontroller electronics, signals take the form of a voltage or current that is produced by a sensor. The signal that is produced by a sensor is usually not in a form we can directly get information from, as we lack the faculties to process sensor information. The microcontroller would need to read the sensor for us, then via a display of some sorts relay the information in a way we can understand. The microcontroller can also take this information and perform some action. For example, a digitally controlled oven may have a thermocouple sensor to read the temperature inside the oven. The microcontroller would need to switch off a heater when the temperature inside the oven reaches a preset temperature. This is just one application where an ADC module may be utilized.

ADC Hardware

There are several ways to perform analog to digital conversion, the most common of which is by using the *successive approximation ADC circuit*. A successive approximation ADC uses various circuit components. These components used by the successive approximation circuit include a digital to analog converter (DAC) that converts a digital signal into an analog one. It also uses a comparator, a sample and hold (S&H) circuit, and a control circuit, which we'll go through in a moment. The successive approximation ADC circuit looks something like Figure 6-1.

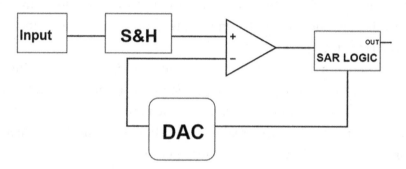

Figure 6-1. *Successive Approximation Circuit*

The circuit operates by first taking an input from the microcontroller pin. Since there is only one ADC module on a typical microcontroller, using a multiplexer circuit, we can route the voltage from several pins to the ADC module within the microcontroller. This is because one module can only read one pin at a time, and many times, we may need our microcontroller to read several sensors.

To ensure that the ADC functions correctly, a snapshot of the voltage of the microcontroller pin is taken. This snapshot is needed to be taken since the sensor would keep continuously outputting data, and the ADC circuit would need time to perform the conversion. This snapshot is taken at that point in time the ADC module is invoked to perform the conversion by the microcontroller. To take the snapshot, a capacitor is used because, as we learned before, a capacitor can store voltage. The capacitor will be charged up to the same voltage value as the pin we want to read the voltage of. For example, if a sensor outputs 3.7 volts, then quickly outputs 3.9 volts, then 4.0 volts, we need some sequence to effectively digitize all these readings. This is because a lone ADC module lacks the ability to perform parallel conversion. The ADC module would first need to take the 3.7 volts, convert it to digital form, then the 3.9 volts, and so forth.

This voltage that the capacitor is charged to will be what we will use to perform the successive approximation procedure on the microcontroller. We call this front end on the ADC module with the capacitor a sample and hold (S&H) circuit.

Once there is a voltage on the S&H circuit, the comparator working together with the ADC circuit comes into action. The combination of these two circuits will keep cutting the voltage at the input in half. When we say the voltage at the input, we are really talking about the snapshot voltage. The process will continue until we reach as close to the input value as the combination of these circuits will allow.

When discussing ADC, a word that comes up frequently is resolution. Let's take a closer look about what is meant by resolution. The ADC module has a range of values that it can use to represent the converted signal. This value is represented as a number of binary bits which is output by the module. Essentially, the smallest voltage which causes a bit change is what we refer to as the resolution. According to the resolution of the ADC, the ADC module will have a certain number of voltage steps that it can use to represent the voltage measured. The greater the number of voltage steps, the greater the resolution of the ADC module.

To output the information, the ADC circuit will manipulate the most significant bit (MSB) down to the least significant bit (LSB) of the binary number which is to be output by the module using the conversion value from the comparator and DAC. This is to try to match the voltage value read on the input as closely as possible and represent it in binary form. This output value is of course limited by the resolution of the DAC within the ADC module. This is because the amount of times the voltage can be cut is dependent on the DAC resolution. This value is then output from the ADC module so that it can be read and manipulated by the CPU.

When selecting a microcontroller for your application, sometimes the resolution of the ADC can be a deciding factor in selection of your device. The resolution required to read a temperature or light sensor, for example, may not be as important. However, if we need to build a circuit for voice recognition, you will need high resolution to have a functional circuit. ADC circuits onboard the microcontroller typically have a resolution of about 8 to 16 bits. For most sensor reading applications, this is sufficient, and if greater resolution is required, for example, in specialized medical applications, an external ADC IC is used.

Going Deeper into ADC

At this point, we will look at some additional terms you are likely to encounter when discussing ADC. The first thing we need to talk about when discussing ADC is sampling. As we explained in the previous section, in order for the ADC module to have time to process the read value, a snapshot of the voltage must be taken. Sampling is the name given to the number of snapshots we can take over a period of time. When we talk about sampling in analog to digital conversion, what we are talking about is the ability of the ADC module to replicate the signal it is analyzing and create a digital equivalent as close to the original as possible. The more samples a digital to analog converter can capture, the more accurate the digital representation of the original signal will be.

A dilemma you may arrive at is trying to determine the optimal amount of samples we need to take to have a decent representation of the signal we are sampling. If we take a lot of signals, then our module will be slow and may not have the response time we need for our application. On the other hand, if we take too few samples, we will have a fast conversion; however, we may not have an accurate representation of the original signal. A special sampling rate known as the Nyquist sampling rate is the benchmark that is used to determine the minimum sampling time.

The Nyquist sampling rate is stated as having the minimum sampling rate being at least twice the highest frequency of the signal we are trying to sample. For example, if a signal is expected to have a maximum frequency of 10 kHz, then we must have a minimum sampling rate of 20 kHz. Another way of saying it is that the sample and hold circuit must take 20,000 snapshots a second to adequately measure the signal.

ADC modules also have a data sampling rate that is usually measured in the number of samples per second (SPS) the ADC module is capable of measuring. Typically, we would see the manufacturer specifying the sampling rate in kilo samples per second (kSPS) or mega samples per second (MSPS).

Another facet we can look at within ADC conversion is that of quantization. Quantization is the name given to the process of mapping the value of input voltage to the ADC to an output value that the ADC is capable of producing. A 10-bit ADC module, for example, will have steps from 0 to 1023. We call this value from 0 to 1023 the quantization level of the ADC. An 8-bit ADC will have quantization levels from 0 to 255. This quantization is the name given to the rounding of values that are equal to the voltage we tried to measure on the pin. What this means is that in the strictest sense we can redefine resolution to mean the measure distance between two adjacent quantization levels.

The Potentiometer

The first device we will look at for using with the ADC module is the potentiometer. When we look at real-world embedded devices, you will realize that potentiometers are found in a lot of devices. For example, the volume knobs that are encountered on stereos and speaker systems use potentiometers in order to allow the user to make adjustments to the volume on these devices. Such devices all use potentiometer circuits to operate properly. In Figure 6-2, we see what a potentiometer looks like.

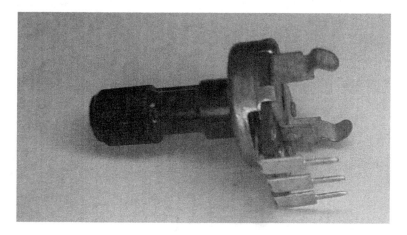

Figure 6-2. *The Potentiometer*

The potentiometer may come in varying form factors; however, if we look at its mechanical construction, we will observe that they are all three-pin devices with a turning mechanism at the top to allow for adjustment. Sometimes, you may see a device looking like a potentiometer with five or more pins protruding from it. This is not a potentiometer but is a rotary encoder and functions differently.

Of the three pins on the potentiometer, one pin is connected to the supply rail, the other pin is connected to the ground supply, and the third pin is connected to the input pin of the microcontroller. When you adjust the knob on the potentiometer, what you are doing is varying the voltage on the analog input from 0 volts to VDD. This can typically range from 0 volts to 3.3 or 5 volts.

The reason this occurs is because the potentiometer can be thought of as a type of voltage divider circuit. A voltage divider is a circuit that turns a larger voltage into a smaller one using the properties that exist when two resistors are placed in series. In Figure 6-3, we see what this voltage divider arrangement looks like.

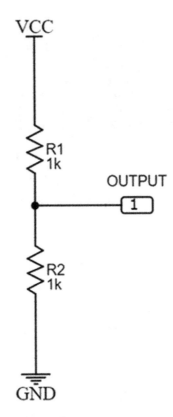

Figure 6-3. *The Voltage Divider*

The voltage divider as shown in Figure 6-3 will output approximately half of the voltage that is present on VCC. So if VCC is 5 volts, then the output of the voltage divider will be 2.5 volts. The output of the voltage divider is determined to be the voltage measured at the center point of both resistors. This is what voltage dividers do; they output a fraction of the input voltage that is present on the input. The output of the voltage divider is not arbitrary but is determined based on the values of the resistors that make up the divider circuit. Once we know the value of the resistors, we can use what is known as the voltage divider formula to calculate the output. This formula is useful when we need to get a specific voltage output using resistors.

To calculate the output of the voltage divider, we use the formula which is given as

$$Vout = Vin(R2/(R1 + R2)$$

We know that the divider circuit in Figure 6-3 would give half the input voltage; however, if we wanted to calculate the same mathematically, we can use our voltage divider formula. If we wanted to calculate our Vout, we could use the formula and input the values of our Vin, R1, and R2. When performing our calculation, we take R1 to be the top resistor and R2 to be the resistor on the bottom, and we get

$$Vout = 5v\,(1 / (1 + 1)) = 5v \times 0.5 = 2.5$$

The potentiometer functions as a resistor and exhibits resistance. However, it can be thought of as a different device entirely, and as such it is given its own schematic symbol. We see the schematic symbol for the potentiometer in Figure 6-4.

Figure 6-4. *The Potentiometer Schematic Symbol*

The schematic symbol for the potentiometer consists of an arrow pointing to a resistor. This is meant to indicate that the resistance is adjustable. Sometimes, you see a smaller version of the potentiometer as shown in Figure 6-5.

Figure 6-5. *The Trimmer Potentiometer*

This version of the potentiometer is called a trimmer potentiometer or a trim pot. The function is the same as the regular potentiometer; however, it is designed to be hidden in the end product and adjusted by the manufacturer or service personnel, not by the end user of the product. These are easy to identify because whereas a regular potentiometer has the adjustment knob extended out from the device, these must be adjusted by a screwdriver in order to change their values.

Analog to Digital Conversion in CircuitPython

CircuitPython provides libraries for working with ADC. The libraries we will be working for analog to digital conversion are

- board – The board module contains the pin constants for the board we are using.

- analogio – This is the module that contains all the classes that provides access to both analog input and output functions we are using. This is the module that allows us to read analog data from our analog capable pins.

- time – The time library contains functions that will allow the microcontroller to use time-related functions. The sleep method is the one we will utilize to aid with timing for our microcontroller.

Note   Some boards may not support some functionality such as analog input functionality particularly if their firmware is in beta; for that reason, it is best to check the release notes for the board you are using.

ADC with MCU Schematic

The potentiometer can be connected to our MCU as shown in Figure 6-6.

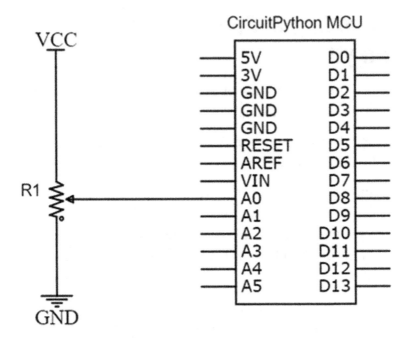

Figure 6-6. *MCU with Potentiometer*

ADC Circuit Connection Tips

These are the recommended steps to connect the circuit:

1. Connect a jumper wire from the A0 pin on your microcontroller to a socket on the prototyping area of your breadboard.

2. Connect the center lead of the resistor to another socket in the same row of the breadboard used in step 1.

3. Take a jumper wire and connect it from one lead of the potentiometer to VCC.

4. Connect the last lead of the potentiometer to the ground with a jumper wire.

When you have finished connecting the circuit, it should look similar to Figure 6-7.

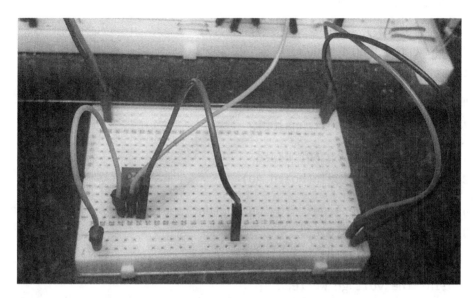

Figure 6-7. *MCU with Potentiometer Breadboard*

Once you have your circuit setup, we run the program as shown in Listing 6-1. Remember to check your connections and ensure they are in accordance with your schematic, or else you risk damaging your board circuit components. For that reason, I always recommend you connect your circuits with the power off, then power it on before writing your program to test it.

CircuitPython with Potentiometer Program

Now that we have connected the physical circuit, we can look at how to read the potentiometer using CircuitPython. Edit your code.py file in the Mu editor to reflect Listing 6-1.

Listing 6-1. MCU with Potentiometer Program

```
# import time module
import time

# import the board module
import board

# import our analog read function
1 from analogio import AnalogIn

# read the A0 pin on our board
2 analog_in = AnalogIn(board.A0)

# get the voltage level from our potentiometer
3  def get_voltage(pin):
     return (pin.value * 3.3) / 65536

# print the voltage we read
4  while True:
     print((get_voltage(analog_in),))
     time.sleep(0.1)
```

The first thing we do is import the CircuitPython libraries we need to control the board. These are our usual imports of our time and board libraries. At (1) we import the AnalogIn object from the analogio module. This is the library that allows us to perform analog functions. The next step in our program at (2) is to create a pin object that will allow us to read the specific analog pin we are working with. In this case, we are working with pin A0 on the board, and we name it analog_in.

Moving along the program at (3), we then have a function that allows us to read the voltage level from our potentiometer. This function get_voltage will take a pin as the input and then will perform calculations to return the correct potentiometer reading. At (4) in our super loop, we use the get_voltage function to read our analog input pin and continuously print this read voltage to our serial console. Once everything is running okay, in your serial console, you should see the output as in Figure 6-8.

Figure 6-8. *MCU with Potentiometer Output*

When we adjust the input of the potentiometer, we see that the output goes from 0 volts to around 3.3 volts, and this value is printed to the serial terminal.

Photoresistor

One sensor that we will now be able to use thanks to this ability to read analog sensors is the photoresistor. A photoresistor is a type of resistor that changes resistance based on the amount of light that is falling on them. When there is no light falling on the photoresistor, it has an extremely high resistance in the order of hundreds of kiloohms. However, when light falls on the photoresistor, the resistance drops to a few hundred ohms.

To create a program to read the photoresistor, we will need to create a voltage divider circuit. This voltage divider circuit will consist of the photoresistor with a regular resistor. The output of the circuit will then be read by the microcontroller to determine change in the light levels of the photoresistor.

Photoresistor with MCU Schematic

We connect the circuit as is shown in Figure 6-9. We have the photoresistor connected to pin A1 and an LED connected to pin A2.

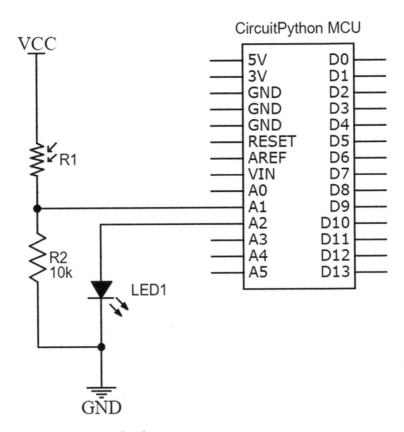

Figure 6-9. *MCU with Photoresistor*

Photoresistor Circuit Connection Tips

These are the recommended steps to connect the circuit:

1. Connect a jumper wire from the A2 pin on your microcontroller to a socket on the prototyping area of your breadboard to one lead of the LED.

2. Connect the other lead of the LED to the ground with a jumper wire.

3. Take a jumper wire and connect one lead of the photoresistor to VCC.

4. Connect the other lead of the photoresistor to one lead of the 10k resistor.

5. Take a jumper wire and connect the other lead of the 10k resistor to the ground.

6. Run a jumper wire from the intersection of the resistor and photoresistor to pin A1 on your microcontroller.

When you have finished connecting the circuit, it should look like Figure 6-10.

Figure 6-10. *MCU with Photoresistor Breadboard*

Now that we have our circuit setup, we can write some code!

Photoresistor with CircuitPython Program

Edit your code.py in the Mu editor so that it resembles Listing 6-2.

Listing 6-2. MCU with Photoresistor Program

```
# import the board module
import board

# import time library
import time

# import our analog read function
from analogio import AnalogIn

# import pin control
import digitalio
```

```
# set an adjust value
1 adjustValue = 2000

# create object for pin we are using
2  led = digitalio.DigitalInOut(board.A2)

# set the pin to output
3 led.direction = digitalio.Direction.OUTPUT

# read the A1 pin on our board
4 photoresistor = AnalogIn(board.A1)

# set an ambient light value
5 ambientLightValue = photoresistor.value

# release the pin for other use
6 photoresistor.deinit()

# print the voltage we read
7 while True:
    # read the photoresistor
    photoresistor = AnalogIn(board.A1)
    # if bright turn the LED off
    if (photoresistor.value > ambientLightValue - 2000):
        led.value = False
    # turn the LED on
    else:
        led.value = True

    # release the pin for other use
    photoresistor.deinit()
```

This program does a lot of things. Let's look at them to see what happens. At the top of the program, we import our board, time, analogio, and digitalio libraries. At (1) we create an adjustValue variable that is used to aid in the reading of the photoresistor. Our next step is to create an object that represents our real-world LED at (2) and set it to an output at (3). We then create an object to represent our photoresistor at (4). At (5) we then take a single reading from the photocell and store that value. This is the value of the ambient light that currently exists.

Note that after taking our reading, we must use the `deinit` method at (6) to allow our pin to be used in other parts of the program. If we don't do this, then we won't be able to use the pin in our super loop.

Inside our super loop at (7), we continually read the photoresistor value. There is a conditional that checks to see if there is darkness on the LED. If there is darkness, the LED will be turned on, and when there is light, we will turn the LED off.

Save the program and run it. You will observe that when you cover the photoresistor with your hand, the LED turns on; however, when the LED is at ambient brightness or brighter, the LED will not be lit.

Temperature Sensor

One sensor that we can use now that we have access to using analog inputs is a temperature sensor. The temperature sensor we will be using is the TMP36 temperature sensor that gives us temperature readings in Celsius using voltage as an output. The TMP36 is pictured in Figure 6-11.

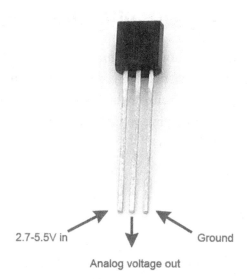

2.7-5.5V in   Ground

Analog voltage out

Figure 6-11. *TMP36 Temperature Sensor Credit: Adafruit, adafruit. com*

The TMP36 temperature sensor device has three pins. One is the VCC pin which we connect to our positive supply. There is also a GND pin which we connect to our ground and an analog voltage out pin which is read by the microcontroller. Depending on the value of the voltage at VCC, the microcontroller can then do some calculations to determine the temperature we are reading.

The sensor works from 2.7 to 5.5v, making it a very versatile sensor as it works with all common microcontrollers equipped with an ADC module. It is capable of being used with CircuitPython-based MCUs that are 3.3-volt devices, which fall within the voltage range of the device. The temperature sensor can take measurements from –50 degrees Celsius to 125 degrees Celsius which is a good range for most projects you will undertake.

Temperature Sensor with MCU Schematic

We connect the circuit as is shown in Figure 6-12. Our TMP36 is connected to our A0 analog input pin. We need the capacitor C1 and resistor R1 to get accurate reading from the sensor when working with a CircuitPython MCU. This is due to the underlying configuration of the device which reads the sensor at a high speed.

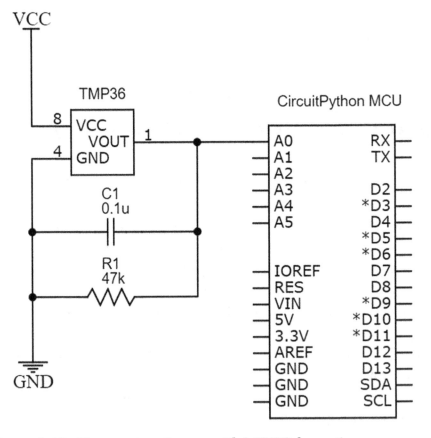

Figure 6-12. *Temperature Sensor with MCU Schematic*

Temperature Sensor Circuit Connection Tips

These are the recommended steps to connect the circuit:

1. Connect a jumper wire from the VCC pin of your TMP36 temperature sensor to the positive rail of your breadboard.

2. Take a jumper wire and connect the ground pin of your sensor to the ground rail of your breadboard.

3. Connect one lead of the 47k resistor to the output pin of the TMP36 sensor and connect the other lead of the resistor to the ground pin of the sensor.

4. Connect one lead of the capacitor to the ground pin and the other lead to the output pin of the TMP36 sensor.

5. Run a jumper wire from the output pin of the temperature sensor to pin A0 on the MCU running CircuitPython.

When you are finished connecting your circuit, it should look similar to Figure 6-13.

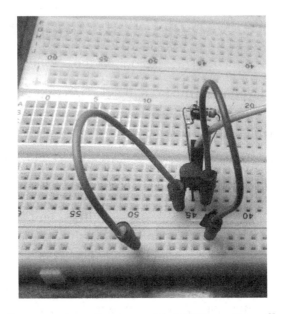

Figure 6-13. *Temperature Sensor with MCU on Breadboard*

Temperature Sensor with CircuitPython Program

Edit your code.py in the Mu editor so that it resembles Listing 6-3. This example is modified from the example provided by Adafruit Industries for reading the sensor.

Listing 6-3. MCU with Temperature Sensor Program

```
# import the board module
import board

# import the time module
import time

# import module for reading analog input
import analogio
```

```
# sensor connected to pin A0
1 TMP36_PIN = board.A0

# function for reading the temperature sensor
2 def tmp36_temperature_C(analogin):
    # convert the voltage to a temperature
    millivolts = analogin.value * (analogin.reference_voltage *
    1000 / 65535)
    return (millivolts - 500) / 10

# create instance of analog object for sensor
3 tmp36 = analogio.AnalogIn(TMP36_PIN)

# super loop
4 while True:
    # read temperature in Celsius
    temp_C = tmp36_temperature_C(tmp36)
    # use Celsius to get Fahrenheit value
    temp_F = (temp_C * 9/5) + 32

    # print our temperature
    print("Temperature: {}C {}F".format(temp_C, temp_F))

    # every second
    time.sleep(1.0)
```

In the program, we do our usual imports to get the board up and running. At (1) we set up the temperature sensor connected to the analog input pin A0. At (2) we have a function for reading the temperature sensor and doing the conversions from voltage to temperature. At (3) we create an instance of the analog object for the temperature sensor. In the main program, we run a super loop at (4) where we read the sensor data and print it to the output consoles every second. If you look at your serial console, you should get an output similar to the output I got in Figure 6-14.

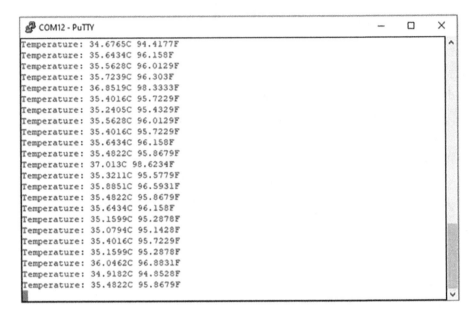

Figure 6-14. *Temperature Sensor Output*

Conclusion

In this chapter, we covered the basics of analog to digital conversion. We looked at how microcontroller ADC circuits work in hardware, and along the way of learning how these circuis function we discovered how potentiometers, photoresistors and voltage dividers work. We also learned how to use CircuitPython with analog inputs. Using this information, we were able to read a temperature sensor and output the information to a serial terminal. With the knowledge gained here, hundreds of sensors are now at your disposal.

CHAPTER 7

Communication Protocols

In the last chapter, we looked at using our microcontroller to read sensors using the analog to digital converter onboard the microcontroller. However, the variety of devices we can interface to our microcontroller can be drastically increased when we start working with serial communications. In this chapter, we will look at the serial communication protocols of UART, SPI, and I2C. Understanding these protocols will expand the interfacing capability of our microcontroller.

Microcontroller Communications

Before we begin looking at specific communication protocols on the microcontroller, let's talk about microcontroller communications in general. On microcontroller systems, there are two types of communication. There is serial communication and parallel communication. A parallel communication system utilizes multiple signal lines to transfer data. Parallel communication is fast and was the preferred method to transfer data in older computing systems. This was due to lack of speed of the processors in these older devices, which were not able to handle the overhead associated with serial communication. When we speak about overhead, we are referring to software overhead which is the additional time the CPU spends doing excess work.

© Armstrong Subero 2021
A. Subero, *Programming Microcontrollers with Python*,
https://doi.org/10.1007/978-1-4842-7058-5_7

In serial communication, data is sent as a stream of bits over much fewer communication lines than a parallel system. While serial communication is slower than parallel communication, if the rate of data transfer is equal, modern hardware is fast enough to eliminate the need for parallel systems. This is not to say that parallel communication is obsolete. Devices like displays, for example, benefit from the higher rate of transfer gained from using parallel communication.

Parallel communication is nowadays reserved for communicating with devices that are within close range of each other. This is because transferring data over a parallel bus would require a lot of additional hardware. For example, wires that make up the transfer lines would require the use of additional resources. Hence, whenever we are transferring data over long distances, we tend to use serial communications.

There exists a myriad of serial communication methods today. Some are simple, while others employ complex protocols that are robust enough to be used in aerospace and automotive applications.

USART Communications

Before we delve further in the section, we should take some time to discuss serial communication. Serial communications can take place in two ways: either asynchronously or synchronously.

Asynchronous communications send data as a stream of bits. This stream of bits usually comprises three parts. At the head of the stream is a start bit that indicates when data has started transmitting. There is also a stop bit at the end that indicates when the data has stopped the transmission. In between the start and stop bits, there is a data packet that contains the data we want to transmit. A data packet is the name we give to a byte of formatted data. The need to send start and stop bits adds a bit of software overhead, which limits the speed at which the transmission can take place. However, these start and stop bits are necessary to allow synchronization between the devices communicating.

Synchronous serial communications remove the overhead associated with sending start and stop bits and thus require less software overhead. This is accomplished by using a clock to synchronize the data transfer. This method, nevertheless, does require an additional line to carry the clock signal. So, while it does make transferring data more efficient, it requires extra hardware to operate properly.

So far, throughout our projects, we have been utilizing serial communication in the form USART communication without realizing it. USART is a serial communication protocol that stands for universal synchronous asynchronous receiver-transmitter. Every time we use PuTTY on our machines to talk to our CircuitPython microcontroller, we are utilizing the power of USART.

Though it is a protocol that is capable of being used synchronously, those features are rarely utilized, and the vast majority of UART communication you encounter in microcontroller-based systems are used asynchronously. For that reason, USART is commonly called UART (universal asynchronous receiver-transmitter), omitting the synchronous bit from the acronym. For that reason, we will focus on the asynchronous method of communication.

Asynchronous UART has two communication lines which are connected to the transmit (TX) pin and a receive (RX) pin. These pins are shared between the transmitter that is sending the data and the receiver that is the recipient of this transferred data. For the data communication to be successful, there must also be a common ground connection between the devices.

Since there is no clock line to aid in the transfer of data via asynchronous UART, the receiver and transmitter must agree on a data transfer rate. This data transfer rate is called the baud rate. The baud rate measures the number of bits that are transferred per second. Most low-level communication interfaces use a baud rate of 9600 baud. The baud rate on your CircuitPython UART interface is around 115,200.

A UART module can operate in three modes of communication which are simplex, half-duplex, and full-duplex communication methods. To understand how these work, imagine we have the UART communication system set up as in Figure 7-1.

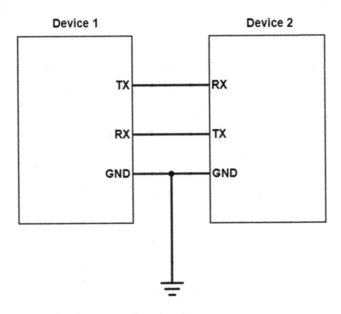

Figure 7-1. *UART Communication System*

If we have data transfer from Device 1 to Device 2 in one direction, this is known as simplex communication. If data is transferred from Device 1 to Device 2, then from Device 2 to Device 1, but not at the same time, then this is known as half-duplex communication. If data is transferred from Device 1 to Device 2, then from Device 2 to Device 1 simultaneously, this is known as full-duplex communication.

Deeper into UART

The stream of bits we talked about earlier within the context of UART is called a data frame. The data frame is the name we give to a single data transmission unit. If we look at the UART data frame, we will see that it consists of 1 start bit, 5 to 9 data bits, 0 to 1 parity bits, and 1 to 2 stop bits. When we put all this together, the UART data frame resembles the arrangement as shown in Figure 7-2.

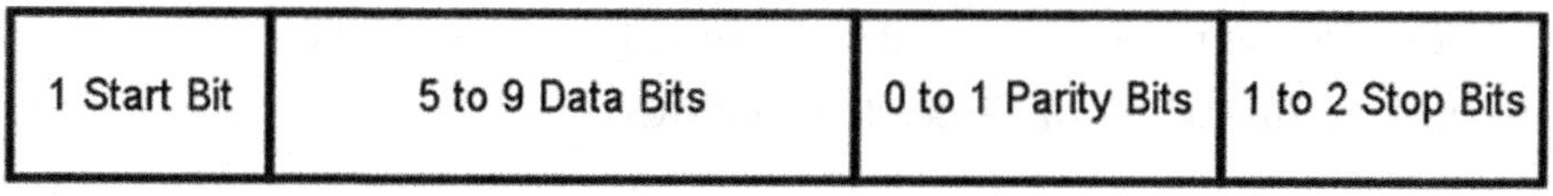

1 Start Bit	5 to 9 Data Bits	0 to 1 Parity Bits	1 to 2 Stop Bits

Figure 7-2. *UART Data Frame*

We know that the purpose of that start bit is to indicate the commencement of the data transfer and that the stop bit indicates when data transfer will stop. However, you may be wondering what the purpose of the parity bit is. The reason for that parity bit is to aid in error detection.

Asynchronous UART has the possibility that interference can take place. When we talk about interference, what we mean is that some factor may cause data corruption and errors in the data transmission. The parity bit is used to aid such scenarios. The parity bit is added to the data packet before the stop bit. Adding this parity bit makes it so that the number of 1s in the data frame is either even or odd. When the packet reaches the destination, if the data frame differs from the expected even or odd value, then we know there is an error in the transmission. Using this information, the packet can then be resent or discarded.

UART in CircuitPython

Within CircuitPython, there are facilities to use onboard hardware peripherals for serial communications, or you can use software routines by a process known as bit banging to perform the serial communications. Since using the hardware peripherals is more efficient, this is the method we will use to control the serial devices.

CircuitPython provides the "busio" library that supports hardware peripherals for UART, SPI, and I2C communications.

These are the modules we will be using to perform UART communications with our CircuitPython MCU:

- board – The board module contains the pin constants for the board we are using.

- time – The time library contains functions that will allow the microcontroller to use time-related functions. The sleep method is the one we will utilize to aid with timing for our microcontroller.

- busio – This is the library that contains functions that allow us to use the CircuitPython facilities for controlling hardware.

USB-UART with MCU Schematic

We connect our microcontroller as shown in Figure 7-3. We can use a USB to UART converter that will allow us to connect the microcontroller to our computer.

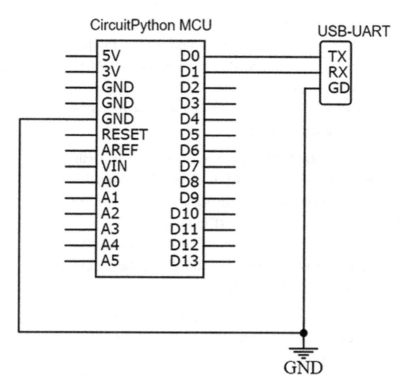

Figure 7-3. *MCU with UART*

MCU with USB-UART Circuit Connection Tips

These are the recommended steps to connect the circuit:

1. Firstly, it is best to keep your circuit powered off when doing the connections for serial communication since a wrong connection can cause damage to your computer USB port.

2. Connect your MCU to the USB to UART module
    with jumper wires as follows. Take the first jumper
    wires and connect the RX pin on your USB-UART
    module to the TX pin of the microcontroller and the
    TX pin of your USB-UART module to the RX pin of
    your microcontroller.

3. If your USB-UART module is a 5-volt one, you will
    have to connect the MCU to the module through a
    logic level converter. To do so, connect the RX and
    TX pins of your USB-UART module to the HL pins
    on your logic level converter, and connect the RX
    and TX pins of your microcontroller to the LV pins of
    your logic level converter.

4. Connect the ground pin on your module to the
    ground pin of your breadboard ground rail with a
    jumper wire.

5. After you have connected everything, double check
    your connections, then power up your circuit.

When you have finished connecting the circuit, it should look like
Figure 7-4.

Figure 7-4. *MCU Connected to USB-UART Breadboard*

UART with CircuitPython Program

Once your circuit is connected, edit your code.py file in the Mu editor to reflect Listing 7-1.

Listing 7-1. Our Program

```
# import the board module
import board

# import time library
import time

# import library for working with UART
  1   import busio
```

```
#setup uart 9600 baudrate, 8 bits, no parity, 1 stop
2    uart = busio.UART(board.TX, board.RX, baudrate=9600,
                bits=8, parity=None,
                stop=1, receiver_buffer_size=64)

3    while True:
   # read up to 64 bytes of data
   dataRead = uart.read(64)

   # once we got data print it
   if dataRead is not None:
      print("I got data")
```

Our program is a simple program that is used to verify that the UART module is working. Firstly, we import the board and time libraries to get our board up and running. At (1) we import the busio libraries for working with the UART. At (2) the UART module is then set up with the default RX and TX pins for the board. We also configure the UART to have a value of 9600 baud and 8 bits of data, and we don't perform any parity checking. Additionally, we set 1 stop bit, and we set up a buffer size for the receiver of 64 bytes. These settings are standard UART values. At (3) we have an infinite loop that reads data from the UART module and then lets us know when data is received by the UART module.

When you save the file and the program is run you can begin interacting with your circuit. If you type data over your serial connection to the USB-UART module, your serial terminal will display the message "I got data".

SPI Communications

The next serial communication protocol we will look at is SPI. SPI stands for Serial Peripheral Interface. SPI is another serial communication method used by microcontrollers. Unlike USART that can operate either synchronously or asynchronously, SPI is a synchronous only protocol.

Being synchronous makes SPI a fast protocol since the limit on the speed of the module is usually dependent on the hardware limitations of the module. SPI uses a clock to keep devices synchronized, and the module can run as fast as the clock used for communication will allow.

SPI uses a master and slave relationship for devices that interact with each other. The device that generates the clock is called the master device, and the other device that it is being communicated with is called the slave. The typical SPI module onboard a microcontroller can operate in both master mode and slave mode.

SPI has four lines. The first line is called the Master Out Slave In (MOSI). This line sends data from the master to the slave. The other line is one that sends data from the slave to the master; we call it Master In Slave Out (MISO). There is also a clock line (SCK) which is responsible for carrying the clock signal that keeps the devices synchronized. Finally, there is a slave select (SS) also called the chip select (CS) line. This line has a special purpose. You see the SPI bus can support as many slaves as the slave select line will allow. When the slave select line of a device is selected by the master, the slave will know that it must be selected.

You can see what the typical SPI bus connection looks like in Figure 7-5.

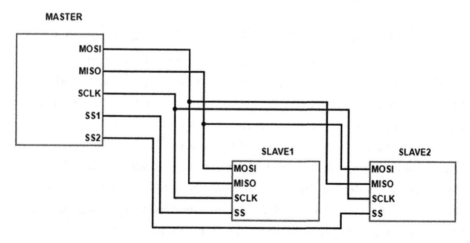

Figure 7-5. *The SPI Bus*

Deeper into SPI

Look at the image in Figure 7-6 so you can get an idea of what SPI communication is like internally.

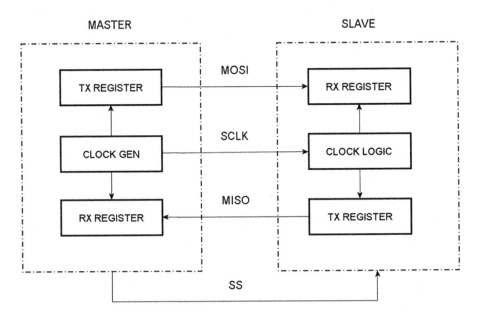

Figure 7-6. *SPI Basic Block Diagram*

SPI works by using several shift registers that convert the parallel data given by them into serial data that can be transmitted via the SPI bus. Recall that we said the master generates the clock. This clock is used as input into all the shift registers located within the module which in turn lets the master control the speed of transmission.

To transmit data, the SPI bus works as follows. The slave select line transitions from high to low to start the transmission. Data is then transferred according to the rising or falling edge of the clock. We call this the clock phase. Based on the clock polarity selected by the user, the SPI module will know when to operate. The clock polarity is the name given to the default state of the clock line, which can be either being high or low during what we call the idle state. The slave select line goes from low to high at the end of the phase.

SPI Circuit Connection

1. Take a jumper wire and connect the MOSI pin on your MCU to the MISO pin.

SPI with CircuitPython Program

After you place a jumper wire from the MISO pin to the MOSI pin, open the Mu editor and edit your program so that it resembles Listing 7-2.

Listing 7-2. Our SPI Loopback Program

```
# import the board module
import board

# import time library
import time

# import library for working with SPI
1   import busio

# setup SPI
2   spi = busio.SPI(board.SCK, board.MOSI, board.MISO)

# lock spi bus
3   while not spi.try_lock():
    pass
```

```
# super loop
4    while True:
         # print numbers 0 to 8 via SPI bus
         for x in range(48, 57, 1):
             # buffer for send
             tx = chr(x)

             # buffer for receive
             rx = bytearray(1)

             # SPI RX_TX
             spi.write_readinto(tx, rx)

             # print sent and received data
             print("tx: " + str(tx))
             print("rx: " + str(rx))

             # sleep for 500 ms
             time.sleep(0.5)
```

The SPI program we are using is what is known as a loopback program. A loopback program is a program in which the sender transmits and receives the message it has transmitted. This loopback program can be used to verify the operation of the SPI bus.

At (1) we use the busio library to work with the SPI hardware peripheral. At (2) we set up the SPI module by creating its instance, simultaneously setting the SCK, MOSI, and MISO pins. At (3) we then need to lock the SPI bus to be able to use. This is one of the requirements of CircuitPython and must be done anytime you wish to use the bus. Within our super loop at (4), we print the numbers 0 to 8 using the SPI module to transmit the characters. Once the characters are sent, we read the characters we have transmitted using the SPI module. Once the characters have been transmitted, we print both the sent and transmitted characters to the serial terminal every 500 milliseconds.

I2C Communications

The last communication protocol we will be looking at is the I2C (Inter-Integrated Circuit) protocol. I2C is a serial protocol that has become extremely popular in recent times. You see I2C requires only two lines for communication. These are a serial clock line (SCL) and a serial data line (SDA). Like SPI, I2C has a master that is responsible for controlling the bus and slave devices it communicates with. Where it differs from SPI in that regard is that any device on the I2C bus can be a master at any point in time. Look at Figure 7-7 and you'll see what the I2C bus looks like.

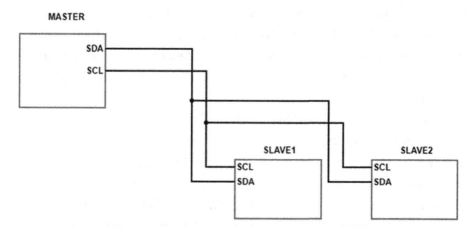

Figure 7-7. *I2C Bus*

As you observe, there is no need for the master to use a slave select line to communicate with I2C devices on a bus. This is because each device on the I2C bus is assigned an address that we can use to read them. This address, which is 7 bits in length, limits the effective range of addresses from 0 to 127, which allows a maximum of 128 devices to be connected to the bus.

Since we lack a slave select line, it is especially important that only the master on the bus initiates communication. If two devices try to initiate communication at the same time, you can get what is known as collisions on the bus. The two lines on the I2C bus are what are known as open-drain pins. Open-drain pins require a pull-up resistor to allow them to be able to output high. For this reason, on the I2C bus lines, a 4.7k pull-up resistor is needed to allow the bus to operate properly.

Deeper into I2C

I2C works by having the data line change states (either HIGH or LOW) when the clock line is low. Data is read when the clock line is high, using start and stop signals that allow for error-free data transfer. Both start and stop conditions are done by keeping the clock line high while changing the level on the data line.

Data is transferred in I2C like in all serial communication protocols, which is by using packets. To ensure that the slave is communicating with the master device, a special acknowledge bit is sent in the packet known as the acknowledge bit. When communicating with a receiver, the transmitting device will release the SDA line. If the line is pulled low, then we will get an acknowledge "ACK" since we know the device is ready to communicate. If not, we will get a not acknowledge "NACK," and we know that the device is not communicating properly.

Figure 7-8 shows us what this I2C transmission sequence looks like.

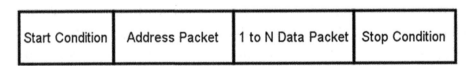

Figure 7-8. I2C Transmission

A new bus that has come into the embedded device scene lately is the System Management Bus (SMBus). SMBus is mainly compatible with I2C except for the fact that it improves upon aspects such as power consumption, timeout requirements, and maximum bus speed.

I2C Support in CircuitPython

CircuitPython provides a library for working with the I2C module onboard the microcontroller. We use the same module that we were using for the UART and SPI module, the busio module.

The MPU6050

The device we will be using to test CircuitPython is the MPU6050. This device combines an accelerometer and a gyroscope in one package which makes it handy for things such as sensor fusion and robotics applications.

The gyroscope within the device measures angular velocity. What this means is that gyroscopes measure the rate of change of the angle of a body which is spinning. Another way of saying this is that gyroscopes essentially measure the rotation of something relative to three axes, which are the X, Y, and Z axes.

The accelerometer in the device measures the rate at which the velocity of an object changes (essentially the force acting on a body). This is usually measured in G-forces or meters per second per second (or m/s squared).

The MPU6050 also includes an onboard temperature sensor that we can use for reading temperature data.

Since the device is in an SMD package, when working with the device, it is common to use it on a breakout board. A breakout board is the name given to a special circuit board that allows us to easily connect to SMD devices like the MPU6050, by providing external pads. We see one such MPU6050 breakout board pictured in Figure 7-9.

Figure 7-9. *MPU6050 BreakoutCredit: Adafruit, adafruit.com*

The data from the accelerometer and gyroscope can be combined in a process we call sensor fusion. When we fuse sensor data from the accelerometer and gyroscope, we get what is known as an inertial measurement unit or IMU. IMUs typically use software filters to mesh this data together. This type of filter is essentially a mathematical operation performed on sampling some data over points in time. There are many methods of doing this filtering, including complementary filters, Kalman filters, and the Madgwick filter. Each filter has its strengths and weaknesses, which you can decide on based on your application. We do not cover sensor fusion in this book; however, you can feel free to explore using various filters on the data we read from the MPU6050 if you so desire.

I2C with MCU Schematic

We connect the MPU6050 to the MCU as shown in Figure 7-10. We must ensure that we include our pull-up resistors. Note that a value between 1k and 10k will work with 4.7k being a nice optimal value.

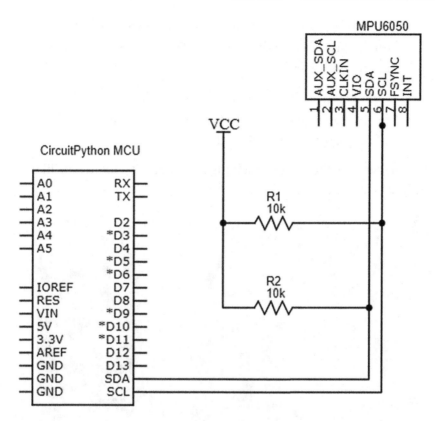

Figure 7-10. *MCU Connected to MPU6050 Schematic*

I2C Circuit Connection Tips

These are the recommended steps to connect the circuit:

1. Firstly, we connect one lead of each of our resistors to VCC.

2. Connect the other lead of each resistor as follows. Connect the free lead of the first resistor to the SCL line and the free lead of the other resistor to the SDA line.

3. Next, run a jumper wire from the SCL and SDA pins
    on the MPU6050 to the SCL and SDA pins on the
    microcontroller.

4. Connect the VCC pin on the MPU6050 to the VCC
    rail on your breadboard and the GND pin to the
    GND rail of your breadboard.

When you have finished connecting the circuit, it should look like
Figure 7-11.

Figure 7-11. *MCU Connected to MPU6050 Breadboard*

I2C with CircuitPython Program

Open the Mu editor and edit your program so that it resembles Listing 7-3.

Listing 7-3. Our I2C Test Program

```
# import the board module
import board

# import time library
import time
```

```
# import library for working with I2C
import busio

# setup the I2C module
1   i2c = busio.I2C(board.SCL, board.SDA)

# lock the I2C bus
2   while not i2c.try_lock():
    pass

# super loop
3   while True:
    # scan for addresses on the bus
    print("I2C addresses found:", [hex(device_address)
                            for device_address in
                            i2c.scan()])

    # every two seconds
    time.sleep(2)
```

The program we wrote will ensure the sensor is set up properly and that communications are being done with the I2C bus. We perform our usual imports to get the microcontroller running. At (1) we set up for I2C communications, creating an instance of our I2C bus we can work with, having the parameters of the physical I2C pins of the device. At (2) we lock the instance of our bus as this is required by CircuitPython. In our main loop at (3), we keep scanning the I2C bus and print the connected devices to our serial console.

Once the sensor is connected properly, you should see that the MPU6050 connected to the bus that has an address of 0x68 will be printed to our serial console.

Adding Libraries

Detecting that the sensor is there is good; however, we may also want to read sensor data as well. To do this, we must add libraries that have been created to make it easy to interface sensors. Adding libraries for the devices is simple. Firstly, ensure that you download the library bundle available for the device you are using from the Adafruit website, from here:

`https://circuitpython.org/libraries`

Once you have downloaded your library, extract it. Open the "CIRCUITPY" drive connected to your computer and open the lib folder. Place the following files from the library bundle into the lib folder of the "CIRCUITPY" drive to use this section:

- The adafruit_register folder

- The adafruit_bus_device folder

- The adafruit_mpu6050.mpy file

Once you have added these files, you will be ready to move on to the next section.

MPU6050 with CircuitPython Program

Now that we have imported our libraries, we will be able to read the MPU6050. We will read the temperature, gyroscope, and accelerometer data and print it to the serial console. Open the Mu editor and edit the file so that it resembles Listing 7-4.

Listing 7-4. Reading Information from the MPU6050

```
# import the board module
import board

# import time library
import time

# import library for working with SPI
import busio

#import library for working with the MPU6050
import adafruit_mpu6050

# setup I2C
i2c = busio.I2C(board.SCL, board.SDA)

# create instance of MPU6050
mpu = adafruit_mpu6050.MPU6050(i2c)

#super loop
while True:
    #print accelerometer data
    print("Acceleration: X:%.2f, Y: %.2f, Z: %.2f m/s^2" %
    (mpu.acceleration))

    # print gyroscope data
    print("Gyro X:%.2f, Y: %.2f, Z: %.2f degrees/s" % (mpu.gyro))

    # print temperature data
    print("Temperature: %.2f C" % mpu.temperature)

    # print space
    print("")

    # every second
    time.sleep(1)
```

Within the program, we import our libraries for working with the board and the I2C module. At (1) we import the library for working with the MPU6050 sensor. At (2) we set up our I2C modules for the pins on the microcontroller we want to use. At (3) we create an instance of the MPU6050 module that we would like to work with. In our super loop at (4), we use the available methods from our library to print information such as the accelerometer, gyroscope, and temperature data to the console every second.

Conclusion

In this chapter, we looked at using serial communications with CircuitPython. We looked at using UART, SPI, and I2C. We also learned how to use the MPU6050 sensor and read gyroscope, accelerometer, and temperature data from the device. There are so many sensors today that use all the protocols covered in this chapter that you will be able to sense and manipulate almost any data from our physical world.

CHAPTER 8

Display Interfacing

All our circuits thus far have been built without using any displays. We can get feedback on our sensor data using things such as an LED or a buzzer, but to really visualize sensor data, we need a display. While the serial console we have been using so far is a good method to visualize information, you need to have your MCU connected to your computer to get any information from it. Most embedded systems though (calculators, watches, and the like) have a display that is used to give information to the user. In this section, we lay the foundations for making these types of devices by learning about displays.

The Liquid Crystal Display

The first type of display we will learn about is the liquid crystal display or LCD. LCDs are made of special crystals called liquid crystals that react to electricity. The way the LCD works is that the liquid crystals are trapped between layers of glass in a grid formation. Each of these trapped dots is called a pixel. When the electricity passes through them, they have the effect of being able to block light from passing. This blocking of light darkens the display and allows us to make patterns that we recognize as information. This is the premise of how monochrome displays work. We see what such a monochrome LCD looks like in Figure 8-1.

© Armstrong Subero 2021
A. Subero, *Programming Microcontrollers with Python*,
https://doi.org/10.1007/978-1-4842-7058-5_8

Figure 8-1. *Monochrome LCD Credit: Adafruit, adafruit.com*

While monochrome LCDs were popular in the past, today it is more common to have full color LCDs designed into our products. We say they are monochrome because they have varying tones of only one color, usually black. There are also color LCDs which work differently from monochrome ones.

Before we discuss color LCDs, let's take some time to discuss color. Within the realm of light, there are two classes of colors. We call them additive colors and subtractive colors.

The additive colors have the primary colors of red, green, and blue which we represent as RGB. If we have a black background (light is absent) and we add combinations of the additive colors together on this black background, we can get a variety of colors. All the additive colors mixed will give you white.

If, however, we have white background (white light is present), we can remove parts of the white light by adding the colors. Certain colors called subtractive colors can remove other colors from the light. We can add cyan (which removes red), magenta (which removes green), and yellow (which removes blue) to also obtain a myriad of colors. These colors are represented as CMY or (-R, -G, -B). When we combine all the subtractive colors, we get black.

210

Ever wonder why we use the colors CMY for printers? It's because if we have a white sheet (white background) and we remove certain light components from them, we can create the spectrum of colors that we use in print media. Mixing all the CMY colors however does not yield complete black. That is why we must have black ink cartridge in our printers. In the printing process, when we use CMY with black, it is called CMYK where K represents the black component.

Now that we understand color, we can move on to our discussion about displays.

The color display has pixels that are made up of red, green, and blue (RGB) components. The pixels can block certain components of light they must represent, and these are called transmissive LCDs. However, there are displays that emit these colors, and we call these emissive LCDs.

To control these pixels, we use a display controller that can handle all the fine-grained control that is needed to effectively operate the LCD. The display controller itself is a microprocessor-based device that can communicate with our MCU to control the pixels on the display. If we do not have a display controller, then we would have to write code to control each individual pixel on the LCD which would add a lot of complexity and software overhead.

Using a GLCD

We will start our display interfacing by looking at how we can interface a monochrome GLCD. While it was commonplace to use a parallel interface to monochrome displays, today it is common to use a serial communication interface to control these LCDs. The first type of display we will use is the one based on the PCD8544 display driver and uses the SPI communication protocol.

The PCD8544-based LCDs are popular because they were once part of the Nokia 5110 phones, and for that reason, they are sometimes called the Nokia 5110 displays. These displays not only display alphanumeric characters but are also capable of displaying graphics and bitmap images. When an LCD can display graphics as well as alphanumeric characters, this display is sometimes called a graphic liquid crystal display (GLCD).

The display has 84x48 monochrome pixels. Figure 8-2 shows us what the PCD8544 display looks like.

Figure 8-2. *PCD8544-Based LCD Credit: Adafruit, adafruit.com*

Though the display in Figure 8-2 is mounted on a green PCB, sometimes it is common to find the display also printed on a red PCB which functions identically. The display has eight pins whose functions are as follows:

- VCC – Connects to VCC.

- GND – Connects to the ground.

- SCE – Our serial chip enable pin that selects the display when active LOW.

- RST – This pin resets the LCD when it is pulled low.

- D/C – This is the data and command pin which is used to tell the LCD if we are sending data or command to the LCD.

- MOSI – Our Master Out Slave In pin used for SPI communication.

- SCLK – This is the serial clock line used for SPI communication.

- LED – The LED or LIGHT pin powers the backlight on the display.

Monochrome GLCD Schematic

We can now connect the PCD8544-based LCD to our display as in Figure 8-3.

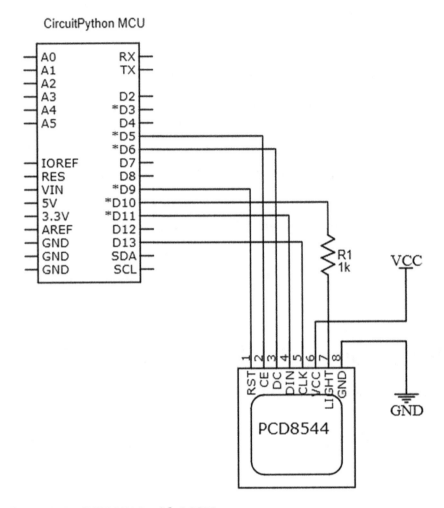

Figure 8-3. *PCD8544 with MCU*

Be sure to check the pinouts for your board related to the SPI MOSI and SPI SCLK lines. Once you have connected the circuit, we can move on to the next step.

1. Take a jumper wire and connect the GND pin of the display to the GND rail of the breadboard.

2. Connect the LED pin to pin D10 on the microcontroller.

214

3. Take a jumper wire and connect the VCC pin on the display to the VCC rail on the breadboard.

4. Connect the LCD clock pin to pin D13 of the microcontroller.

5. Connect the DIN pin to pin D11 of the microcontroller.

6. Take a jumper wire and connect the DC pin on the LCD to pin D6 of the microcontroller.

7. Connect the CE pin on the LCD to pin D5 of the microcontroller.

8. Finally, connect the LCD RST pin to pin D9 of the microcontroller.

PCD8544 with CircuitPython

The PCD8544 device has a library that was written for CircuitPython. To use the LCD with CircuitPython, we must add the following files from the Adafruit libraries bundle to the lib folder on our microcontroller:

- adafruit_pcd8544.mpy

- adafruit_framebuf.mpy

- adafruit_bus_device folder

Once you have added these to your lib folder, then we can write the program given in Listing 8-1.

Listing 8-1. PCD8544 with CircuitPython

```python
# import the board module
import board

# import time library
import time

# import library for working with SPI
import busio

# import library for digital I/O
import digitalio

# import the LCD library
(1) import adafruit_pcd8544

(2) # Initialize SPI bus
spi = busio.SPI(board.SCK, MOSI=board.MOSI)

        #initialize the control pins
dc = digitalio.DigitalInOut(board.D6)
cs = digitalio.DigitalInOut(board.D5)
reset = digitalio.DigitalInOut(board.D9)

# create instance of display
(3) display = adafruit_pcd8544.PCD8544(spi, dc, cs, reset)

(4) # set bias and contrast
display.bias = 4
display.contrast = 60

(5) # Turn on the Backlight LED
backlight = digitalio.DigitalInOut(board.D10)
backlight.switch_to_output()
backlight.value = True
```

```
# we'll draw from corner to corner, lets define all the pair
  coordinates here
(6) corners = (
    (0, 0),
    (0, display.height - 1),
    (display.width - 1, 0),
    (display.width - 1, display.height - 1),
)

(7) #draw some graphics
      display.fill(0)
for corner_from in corners:
    for corner_to in corners:
        display.line(corner_from[0], corner_from[1], corner_
        to[0], corner_to[1], 1)
display.show()
time.sleep(2)

(8) # draw some graphics
display.fill(0)
w_delta = display.width / 10
h_delta = display.height / 10
for i in range(11):
    display.rect(0, 0, int(w_delta * i), int(h_delta * i), 1)
display.show()
time.sleep(2)

(9) # draw text
display.fill(0)
display.text("hello world", 0, 0, 1)
display.show()
```

```
(10) #super loop
while True:
    # invert display
    display.invert = True
    time.sleep(0.5)

    # remove invert
    display.invert = False
    time.sleep(0.5)
```

Our program works as follows. First, we perform our regular imports to set the board up and get it running. At (1) we import the library for working with the LCD. At (2) we initialize the SPI bus and then the control pins. At (3) is where we create the instance of the actual module we will be using. We then go on to set options to control the bias and contrast of the display at (4). The next step is to turn on the backlight LED which we do at (5).

Our next step is to demonstrate the graphics capabilities of the LCD. At (6) we draw corners on the display, at (7) and (8) some nice graphics effects, and at (9) we write some text on the LCD. In the super loop at (10), we demonstrate the library inversion capabilities.

Troubleshooting

At the time of writing, there is an error that may occur if you try to run this program as is. You will see an output complaining about fonts as shown in Figure 8-4.

```
Could not find font file font5x8.bin
Traceback (most recent call last):
  File "code.py", line 45, in <module>
  File "adafruit_framebuf.py", line 362, in text
  File "adafruit_framebuf.py", line 427, in __init__
  File "adafruit_framebuf.py", line 420, in __init__
OSError: [Errno 2] No such file/directory: 'font5x8.bin'
```

Figure 8-4. *Cannot Find Font Error*

The solution to this is to simply place the font file "font5x8.bin" in the root folder of your CIRCUITPY drive as shown in Figure 8-5.

Figure 8-5. *Placing the Font File*

After you have placed the font file, run the program again, and you will see text being output to your display. One of the graphics output from the program will look like what is shown in Figure 8-6.

Figure 8-6. *Circuit on Breadboard*

219

We now have our monochrome LCD working with CircuitPython. In the next section, we will look at extending on what we already know.

The Framebuffer

To make updating a display output more efficient, we can import a library known as "adafruit_framebuf.mpy" which provides framebuffer capabilities. A framebuffer is the name given to holding the frame of data we will be outputting into memory. The framebuffer can not only be used with LCDs but with any output device including the serial terminal. Look at Listing 8-2 where we use the framebuffer to output data to the serial terminal.

Listing 8-2. Framebuffer with CircuitPython

```
# import the frame buffer library
(1) import adafruit_framebuf

print("framebuf test will draw to the REPL")

(2) WIDTH = 32
HEIGHT = 8

(3) buffer = bytearray(round(WIDTH * HEIGHT / 8))
fb = adafruit_framebuf.FrameBuffer(
    buffer, WIDTH, HEIGHT, buf_format=adafruit_framebuf.MVLSB
)

(4) # Ascii printer for very small framebufs!
def print_buffer(the_fb):
    print("." * (the_fb.width + 2))
    for y in range(the_fb.height):
        print(".", end="")
```

```
        for x in range(the_fb.width):
            if fb.pixel(x, y):
                print("*", end="")
            else:
                print(" ", end="")
        print(".")
    print("." * (the_fb.width + 2))
```

(5) ```# Small function to clear the buffer```
```
def clear_buffer():
    for i, _ in enumerate(buffer):
        buffer[i] = 0
```

(6) ```print("Shapes test: ")```
```
fb.pixel(3, 5, True)
fb.rect(0, 0, fb.width, fb.height, True)
fb.line(1, 1, fb.width - 2, fb.height - 2, True)
fb.fill_rect(25, 2, 2, 2, True)
print_buffer(fb)
```

(7) ```print("Text test: ")```
```
# empty
fb.fill_rect(0, 0, WIDTH, HEIGHT, False)

# write some text
fb.text("hello", 0, 0, True)
print_buffer(fb)
clear_buffer()

# write some larger text
fb.text("hello", 8, 0, True, size=2)
print_buffer(fb)
```

The framebuffer example in Listing 8-2 is the one provided in the CircuitPython library bundle and demonstrates how we can use the CircuitPython framebuffer to output to a display. First, we import the framebuffer library at (1). At (2) we set the dimensions of the buffer which we then use to create the buffer at (3). Our next step is to create a function to print the buffer, which we do at (4). At (5) we have a function which clears the buffer. At (6) we print shapes to the serial terminal, and at (7) we print some text followed by some larger text.

When you run the program, you will observe that there is text and shapes in ASCII code written to your serial terminal.

OLED

LCDs are a great technology and have served the technology world for a long time. There is however another display technology that has become popular in the technology world. This is the organic light-emitting diode (OLED)-based display.

OLED displays generate rich crisp color and have a wider viewing angle than traditional LCD displays. They also feature a faster response time. It is easy to tell an OLED display when looking at it compared to an LCD. The colors are much cleaner and clearer due to increased contrast provided by the display. OLED displays have additional layers in their construction when compared to LCD displays. These layers are made of organic substances that allow them to emit light. Think of the OLED like a sandwich as shown in Figure 8-7.

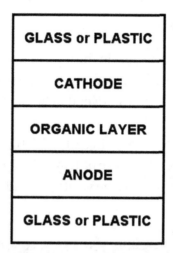

Figure 8-7. *Basic OLED Structure*

The simplified sandwich in Figure 8-7 is a good representation of what an OLED is like. It consists of having an organic layer sitting between anode and cathode material. These are then placed in between a bottom layer made of glass or plastic we call the substrate. The organic layer is, in and of itself, made up of two layers which are the emissive layer and the conductive layer. The OLED emits light by having electricity travel from the cathode layer through the organic layer to the cathode layer. This flow of electricity causes light to be emitted. Due to the OLED being able to emit its own light, there is no need for a backlight like in most LCD displays.

Like the LCD, OLED displays require a driver that will allow us to easily control the OLED, and in the next section, we will look at how we can interface displays to our own microcontroller circuits.

Using an OLED

There are many displays available in the market today; however, sometimes interfacing with the driver can be an issue. For this reason, we will look at using an OLED with a driver that has a library available that we can easily control.

The OLED display we will be using is the SSD1306-based OLED that has 128 x 64 pixels with a screen size of 1.44". Many versions of this display can use both SPI and I2C such as the version provided by Adafruit in Figure 8-8.

Figure 8-8. *SSD1306-Based LCD Credit: Adafruit, adafruit.com*

We will use the display in I2C mode as there are a lot of low-cost I2C-only versions as shown in Figure 8-9.

Figure 8-9. *SSD1306-Based LCD I2C Only*

The I2C mode of the display uses four lines which are VCC, GND, SCL, and SDA. Only the SCL and SDA lines will be used from our MCU, requiring just two I/O lines to drive the OLED.

MCU with OLED Schematic

The schematic involves connecting our OLED to the I2C bus as shown in Figure 8-10. Some versions of the display include the pull-up resistors for the I2C bus; we will still include them just in case your version of the display does not include pull-up resistors.

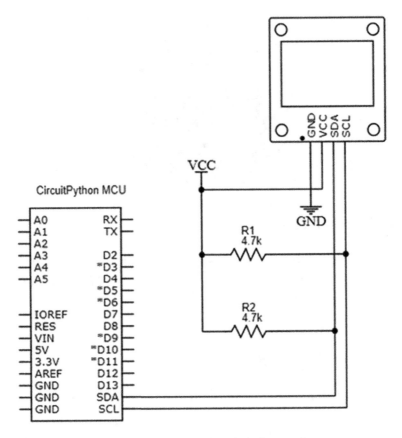

Figure 8-10. *MCU with SSD1306 OLED Schematic*

We connect the display to the microcontroller as follows:

(1) Connect the GND pin on the OLED to the GND pin on the breadboard using a jumper wire.

(2) Take a jumper wire and connect the VCC pin from the OLED to the VCC rail on the breadboard.

(3) Connect the SDA pin on the OLED to the SDA pin of the microcontroller.

(4)   Connect the SCL pin of the OLED to the SCL pin of
the microcontroller.

(5)   Take your resistors and connect them as follows.
Connect one lead of each resistor to the VCC rail
of the breadboard. Take the free leads and connect
one side to the SDA and SCL pins of the OLED,
respectively.

CircuitPython with OLED Program

For our program, we use the example provided by Adafruit to make the
animation of a bouncing ball on the display. The program is given in
Listing 8-3.

Listing 8-3. Bouncing Ball Program

```
# usual imports
import board
import busio

(1) # import library for working with SSD1306
import adafruit_ssd1306

# Create the I2C interface.
i2c = busio.I2C(board.SCL, board.SDA)

(2) # Create the SSD1306 OLED class.
# The first two parameters are the pixel width and pixel
height.  Change these
# to the right size for your display!
oled = adafruit_ssd1306.SSD1306_I2C(128, 64, i2c)
```

(3) # Helper function to draw a circle from a given position

with a given radius

```
# This is an implementation of the midpoint circle algorithm,
# see https://en.wikipedia.org/wiki/Midpoint_circle_
algorithm#C_example for details
def draw_circle(xpos0, ypos0, rad, col=1):
    x = rad - 1
    y = 0
    dx = 1
    dy = 1
    err = dx - (rad << 1)
    while x >= y:
        oled.pixel(xpos0 + x, ypos0 + y, col)
        oled.pixel(xpos0 + y, ypos0 + x, col)
        oled.pixel(xpos0 - y, ypos0 + x, col)
        oled.pixel(xpos0 - x, ypos0 + y, col)
        oled.pixel(xpos0 - x, ypos0 - y, col)
        oled.pixel(xpos0 - y, ypos0 - x, col)
        oled.pixel(xpos0 + y, ypos0 - x, col)
        oled.pixel(xpos0 + x, ypos0 - y, col)
        if err <= 0:
            y += 1
            err += dy
            dy += 2
        if err > 0:
            x -= 1
            dx += 2
            err += dx - (rad << 1)
```

(4) # initial center of the circle

```
center_x = 63
center_y = 15
```

```
# how fast does it move in each direction
x_inc = 1
y_inc = 1
# what is the starting radius of the circle
radius = 8

# start with a blank screen
oled.fill(0)
# we just blanked the framebuffer. to push the framebuffer onto
  the display, we call show()
oled.show()
```
(5) `while True:`
```
    # undraw the previous circle
    draw_circle(center_x, center_y, radius, col=0)

    # if bouncing off right
    if center_x + radius >= oled.width:
        # start moving to the left
        x_inc = -1
    # if bouncing off left
    elif center_x - radius < 0:
        # start moving to the right
        x_inc = 1

    # if bouncing off top
    if center_y + radius >= oled.height:
        # start moving down
        y_inc = -1
    # if bouncing off bottom
    elif center_y - radius < 0:
        # start moving up
        y_inc = 1
```

```
# go more in the current direction
center_x += x_inc
center_y += y_inc

# draw the new circle
draw_circle(center_x, center_y, radius)
# show all the changes we just made
oled.show()
```

In our program, we create a bouncing ball. After we perform our usual imports at (1), we import the library for working with the SSD1306 display. At (2) we create an instance of the SSD1306 class we can manipulate. Since a ball is essentially a filled circle, at (3) we have a function to draw the circle. At (4) we set the parameters of the ball including its dimensions and speed. At (5) the infinite loop draws the bouncing ball to the display. If you look in the Adafruit libraries bundle, you will see other example programs you can use for working with displays.

Conclusion

In this chapter, we looked at interfacing displays. We looked at how we can use both the liquid crystal display (LCD) and the organic light-emitting diode (OLED). Along the way, we looked a little into how LCDs and GLCDs work and learned how we can use the Adafruit buffer library for outputting information to the serial console. With the ability to use displays, you can now display information untethered from your computer. The ability to use sensors combined with the ability to display that information covers the functions of many embedded systems.

CHAPTER 9

Controlling DC Actuators

Microcontrollers can be used to control actuator devices. An actuator is a device that is responsible for making movements. Actuators fall into two groups, which are mechanical and electro-mechanical actuators. In this chapter, we will look at controlling some important electro-mechanical DC actuators. After learning to control actuators, an entire world opens to you. Automatic locks, robots, and CNC machines can be understood more easily, and after you will have the ability to build such devices.

DC Motors

The first type of actuator that you will be using is the DC motor. DC motors are used in a lot of devices ranging from toys, such as RC cars, to appliances and tools such as cordless drills.

These motors operate by having a rotary action when a potential difference (voltage) is applied across their terminals.

There are two types of DC motors, which are brushed DC motors and brushless DC motors. Brushless DC motors have better thermal characteristics and higher efficiency than brushed DC motors. However, the brushed DC motors can be driven in a simpler way, which leads to a lower system cost.

© Armstrong Subero 2021
A. Subero, *Programming Microcontrollers with Python*,
https://doi.org/10.1007/978-1-4842-7058-5_9

The brushed DC motors are the type you are likely to use in your own projects, though later in the chapter we will also look at a type of brushless DC motor known as a stepper motor.

Figure 9-1 shows the typical brushed DC motors that are commonly found in toys and other simple devices.

Figure 9-1. *Brushed DC Motor*

Brushed DC motors, due to their mechanical construction, have a shorter lifetime than brushless motors. This is because brushed DC motors have a component known as the brushes which can wear out over time.

Driving DC Motors

Brushed DC motors should be easy to drive; I mean if you connect a DC motor to a battery, as in Figure 9-2, it should run.

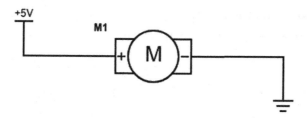

Figure 9-2. *DC Motor with Battery*

This simple method however lacks intelligent control, and the motor will rotate in only one direction. If we want the motor to rotate in the opposite direction under intelligent control, it will require more than just connecting the DC motor with a battery. The way to drive a motor using an MCU will be as in Figure 9-3.

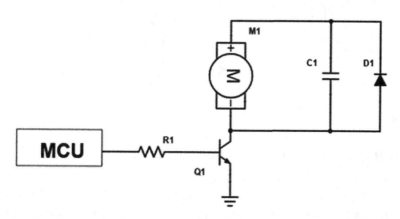

Figure 9-3. *Drive DC Motor with MCU*

The premise of the operation of the circuit is simple. A signal from the microcontroller will cause the transistor to switch on or off. According to the state of the transistor, current will flow through the motor and allow it to rotate. We must remember that a motor is an inductive load. Thus, D1 is a snubber diode which protects other circuit elements from the inductive spike that will be generated by the motor. If you do need simple on/off

control for a small motor such as a vibration motor and the like, then a
nice circuit you can use is the one in Figure 9-4.

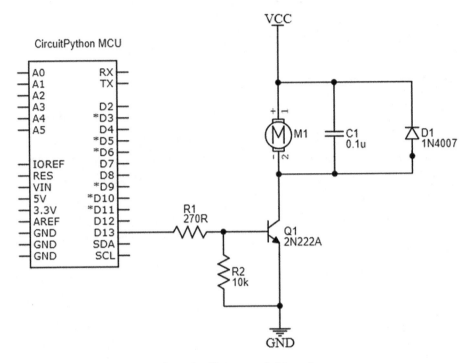

Figure 9-4. *A Practical On/Off Control Circuit*

Here, in Figure 9-4, we have a practical circuit of the version shown
in Figure 9-3. For driving the motor, we use the 2N2222A transistor which
can handle up to 800 mA that is more than sufficient to drive the motor.
Though the 2N3904 is often touted as a replacement for the 2N2222A,
in this circuit it is not suitable since the current handling capability of
the 2N3904 is only 200 mA. This circuit is good if you want to drive small
motors that require simple on/off control. Motors such as a vibration
motor for haptic feedback or the standard 130 DC motor used in toys and
the like as pictured in Figure 9-5 are ideal candidates.

Figure 9-5. *Standard 130 DC Motor Credit: Adafruit, adafruit.com*

While a simple on/off control does have its applications, if we really want an intelligent motor control, we need to have things like direction and speed control. These fall into the domain of pulse width modulation which we will discuss in the next section.

Pulse Width Modulation

If you really want to control the speed of your motor with a microcontroller, then you must look at something called pulse width modulation or PWM. Before we talk about PWM, let's look at the square wave in Figure 9-6.

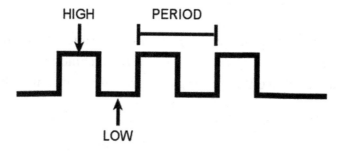

Figure 9-6. *A Square Wave*

On your square wave, you have a time we call the HIGH level time and a time we call the LOW level time. If this square wave was being generated by the microcontroller, we can take the HIGH time to be 3.3 volts and the low time to be 0 volts. The rate at which this pulse repeats is called the frequency of the wave which we measure in hertz (Hz). The period of the wave is an inverse of the frequency and refers to the time it takes for the cycle to repeat itself.

Since the period of the wave is an inverse of the frequency, as the frequency of the waveform increases, there will be a simultaneous decrease in the period of the wave.

An important aspect of PWM is the duty cycle. As we know, a digital signal can be HIGH or LOW. The HIGH time of the waveform is called the duty cycle which is usually expressed as a percentage. For example, if a wave is high half of the time and low half of the time, it can be said to have a duty cycle of 50%.

Figure 9-7 has a diagram showing where we can identify the duty cycle on the waveform.

DUTY CYCLE

Figure 9-7. *The Duty Cycle*

By adjusting the duty cycle of the waveform, we effectively can adjust the voltage level of the output. This is a powerful technique. Using PWM, we can do things like control the brightness of LEDs and control the speed of a motor.

PWM in CircuitPython

Almost every microcontroller today provides a module that is PWM capable, and CircuitPython provides libraries for controlling these PWM modules. Most MCUs that support CircuitPython have PWM pins printed with a little tilde "~" symbol next to the output pin. To use PWM in CircuitPython, we use the following libraries:

- board – We need the board library to indicate which of the specific pins of our microcontroller.

- time – The time library provides functions for working with time-based activities.

- pulseio – The pulseio library is the center of the PWM usage in CircuitPython. This library provides functions for PWM on the pins that support it.

PWM with CircuitPython Program

We can use the PWM module to fade an LED. We can use PWM to fade an LED that is attached to our board. Listing 9-1 has the program we can use to fade the LED attached to a PWM capable pin, in this case pin D13. Most CircuitPython capable boards have an LED connected to this pin; if there is no LED on this pin, or you are using a custom board, then you can connect the LED to pin D13 with a 1k resistor.

Listing 9-1. The PWM Program

```
# import time functions
import time

# import our board specific pins
import board
```

```
# library for using PWM
(1) import pulseio

# setup the pwm using Pin13, with a frequency of 5000 Hz
(2) pwmLed = pulseio.PWMOut(board.D13, frequency=5000)

(3) while True:
    for i in range(100):
        # PWM LED up and down
        if i < 50:
            # below 50 pwm up
            pwmLed.duty_cycle = int(i * 2 * 65535 / 100)
        else:
            # more than 50 pwm down
            pwmLed.duty_cycle = 65535 - int((i - 50) * 2 *
            65535 / 100)
        # slow it down so we can see
        time.sleep(0.05)
```

When you run the program, you will see the LED become very bright and then fade away and become dim. The program works as follows. At (1) we import the "pulseio" library for using PWM. At (2) we create an instance of the PWM module on our pin and set the frequency to 5000 hertz. At (3) we have our main program loop where we increment and then decrement the PWM duty cycle for a specified period. This causes the LED to have a fading effect.

Controlling Motor Speed

If you wish to control a DC motor, the standard way to do this is with PWM control. If we supply the maximum voltage that the motor needs to operate, then the motor will run at full speed. If, however, we turn the motor on and off quickly by adjusting the duty cycle of the motor using PWM, we will be able to control the effective or average speed of the motor.

We can create the hardware connections as shown in Figure 9-8 to control the motor speed.

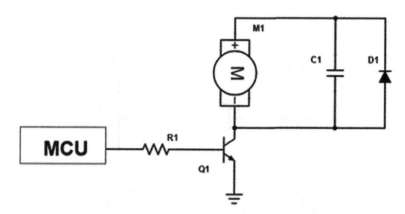

Figure 9-8. *Connection for Motor Control*

This is the same circuit we discussed earlier in the chapter. We simply replace the "MCU" with a pin of your choice and a transistor that can handle the current for the motor you want to control. To control the motor speed, we can use the PWM of the MCU to vary the speed of the motor, using the transistor to do the heavy lifting. There is a better way however that we will look at in the next section.

The H-Bridge

Driving a motor with a transistor is good if you require simple ON/OFF control or just adjusting the speed at which the motor rotates. There are instances however where you wish to adjust not only the speed of your motor, but you require directional control of the rotation as well. A good example of this is in mobile robots. In a mobile robot, the robot will need to not only drive forward but also in the reverse direction. To do this, you would use a circuit configuration known as an H-Bridge as is shown in Figure 9-9.

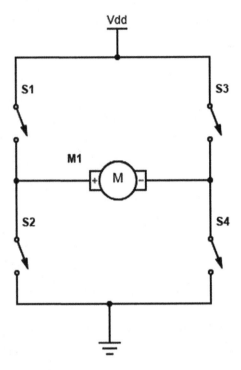

Figure 9-9. *The H-Bridge*

The circuit will work as follows. When S3 and S2 are switched closed, the motor will rotate in a forward direction, and when S1 and S4 are closed, the motor will rotate in a reverse direction. It is important when using an H-Bridge to avoid creating short circuits when driving the motor. If both switches on the left (S1 and S2) or both switches on the right (S3 and S4) are closed, then you will create a short circuit from the source to the ground. If you are using an H-Bridge IC, there is usually thermal shutdown included that would prevent these devices from being destroyed. However, you should not rely on such protection mechanisms to protect your IC.

Usually, it is common to build an H-Bridge from MOSFETs when you require high current handling capability (>5A in this context). For most applications below 5A, however, you would use an H-Bridge IC. It is possible to get IC drivers that handle more than 5A. However, due to the level of power dissipation, as well as the peak current that may be required by the motor, it is usually more economical to build a discrete H-Bridge.

There may be some who may disagree with me, but as semiconductor technology gets better, the need to build your own discrete drivers for most applications will be unnecessary.

For low current applications (<5A in this context), it is common to use an H-Bridge driver IC. Two common H-Bridge ICs are the L293D and the SN754410NE quadruple half-H drivers. These drivers are similar enough that they can be used interchangeably for most applications.

The SN754410NE has a higher continuous current output and a higher peak current than the L293D. Figure 9-10 highlights the difference in characteristics for these both drivers.

Driver	Voltage Range	Continuous Current	Peak Current
L293D	4.5v to 36v	600 mA Channel	1.2A Channel
SN745510NE	4.5v to 36v	1 A Channel	2 A Channel

Figure 9-10. *L293D vs. SN754410NE Characteristics*

In Figure 9-11, we see the physical layouts of both devices. The L293D is on the left, and the SN754410NE is on the right.

Figure 9-11. *L293D vs. SN754410NE Physical Packages*

The packages in Figure 9-11 are PDIP-16 packages, and they are pin compatible with each other. There are VCC supplies for both the chip's internal logic and the motor power supply. VCC1 powers the internal logic of the chip and is connected to 5v, and VCC2 is connected to the motor power supply, usually 9–12v.

The left motor connects to pins 1Y and 2Y, and the right motor will be connected to pins 3Y and 4Y. Pins 1A and 2A are the left logic pins, and the 3A and 4A pins are the right logic pins. The 1,2 EN enables the left driver, and 3,4 EN enables the right driver.

The drivers essentially have three driven states which are forward, reverse, and braking. In the forward state, we set one switch high and the other state low. For reverse rotation, we reverse the logic levels on the pins. To create a braking scenario, we set both logic level pins to a low state.

H-Bridge with MCU Schematic

We can connect the microcontroller to the L293D using a logic level converter since the L293D expects 5v logic, and we have 3.3v devices running CircuitPython. Connect the schematic as in Figure 9-12.

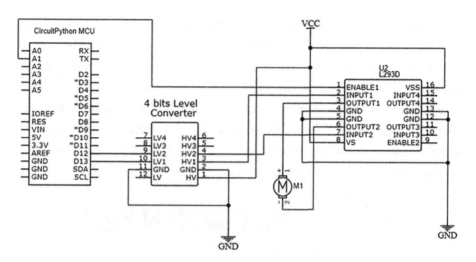

Figure 9-12. *CircuitPython MCU with H-Bridge*

1. Connect pins D12 and D13 from your microcontroller to LV1 and LV2 of your logic level converter.

2. Connect the GND pins on your logic level converter to the ground rail on your breadboard.

3. Connect the HV1 pin of your logic level converter to the INPUT1 pin of your H-Bridge IC and the HV2 pin to the INPUT2 pin.

4. Connect one pin of the motor to OUTPUT1 and the other pin of the motor to OUTPUT2.

5. The enable pin of the H-Bridge is connected to A1 of the MCU.

6. Connect the positive pins of the H-Bridge IC to the power rail and the GND pins to the ground rail.

The connected circuit should look like Figure 9-13. Note that the size of the motor you are using is important as the bigger motors will use more current; as such you must ensure that extra capacitors are placed on the power rails as is seen in Figure 9-13. If you do not place these extra capacitors, then the microcontroller will reset, and you will have an unexpected operation. The ground connections on the right side of the driver are not necessary to be connected for the H-Bridge to operate, but you can connect them as a precaution if you so desire.

Figure 9-13. *H-Bridge with MCU on Breadboard*

H-Bridge with CircuitPython Program

We will write a program that uses PWM to limit the speed of the motor which is driven by a L293D motor driver which will allow us to control the direction of the motor. We will open the Mu editor and create the program in Listing 9-2.

Listing 9-2. Using the H-Bridge

```
# import time functions
import time

# import our board specific pins
import board

# library for using PWM
(1) import pulseio

# library for working with digital output
import digitalio

# create instance of enable pin
(2) en = digitalio.DigitalInOut(board.A1)

# set the enable pin to output
en.direction = digitalio.Direction.OUTPUT

# start with enable false
en.value = False

# setup the pwm using Pin13, with a frequency of 5000 Hz
# steup the pwm using Pin12, with a frequecny of 5000 Hz
(3) in1 = pulseio.PWMOut(board.D13, frequency=5000, duty_
cycle=0)
in2 = pulseio.PWMOut(board.D12, frequency=5000, duty_cycle=0)
```

245

```
# turn in forward direction
(4) def forward():
    print("forward")
    en.value = True
    in1.duty_cycle = 20000
    in2.duty_cycle = 0
    time.sleep(3)

# reverse direction
(5) def reverse():
    print("reverse")
    en.value = True
    in1.duty_cycle = 0
    in2.duty_cycle = 20000
    time.sleep(3)

# stop motors
(6) def stop():
    print("stop")
    en.value = False
    in1.duty_cycle = 0
    in2.duty_cycle = 0
    time.sleep(2)

# super loop
(7) while True:
    # forward
    forward()

    # stop before transition
    stop()

    # reverse
    reverse()
```

```
# stop before transition
stop()
```

In the program, we do our usual imports, and at (1) the pulseio library is imported for working with PWM pins. At (2) the enable pin is set up, and its direction and state are set. At (3) PWM instances are set up which will be used to be interfaced to the H-Bridge. At (4), (5), and (6), functions are created for allowing the motor to rotate forward, to reverse direction, and to stop. The forward function allows the motor to rotate in the forward direction, the reverse function lets the motor rotate in the opposite direction, and the stop function prevents the motor from moving.

In our super loop at (7), we rotate the motor forward for 3 seconds; notice that before we transition to the other direction, we stop the motor for 2 seconds. After that, we reverse the direction of the motor, and this continues indefinitely.

Servo Motors

In the last section, we looked at brushed DC motors and how to drive them. Another common DC actuator you are likely to encounter is the DC servo motor. These servo motors are the R/C (radio control) servo motors since they were intended for use in hobby applications related to remote controls (usually model aircraft).

These motors do not require an external motor driver. This is because they are self-contained having a DC motor with control circuits and a gear train integrated into the device.

These motors have three wires as is shown in Figure 9-14. One wire supplies power to the servo, the other wire is a ground connection, and the last wire is used to send control signals to the motor. The power wire is usually red, the ground wire is brown or black, and the control signal is white or orange.

The servo in Figure 9-14 is the MG90D which is a good standard micro servo to use in your own projects.

There are two types of servos, which are continuous rotation and standard servo motors. Continuous rotation servo motors can rotate a full 360 degrees, whereas standard servos have a range from 0 to 180 degrees.

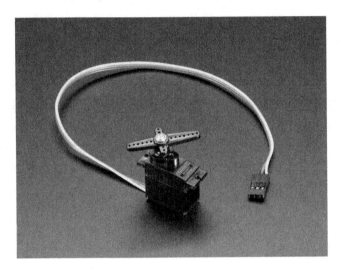

Figure 9-14. *R/C Servo Motor*

To control a servo motor, we need to send a pulse on the signal line. For continuous rotation servos, the length of the pulse will determine how fast the servo rotates. In standard servo motors, the pulse length will determine the position the servo will rotate to.

The pulse length will be specified by the manufacturer. However, for the typical servo, a pulse width of 1 ms will turn the motor to the 0-degree position. When a pulse width of 1.5 ms is supplied, it will cause the motor to turn to the 90-degree position. Finally, when we supply a 2 ms pulse, the motor will turn to a 180-degree position.

The servo motor will also require a signal to be sent to hold its position for any duration of time. If this signal is not sent, the motor may become very irregular in its operation, having jerky movements.

Servo Motors in CircuitPython

Controlling a servo is simple but can be daunting to a beginner. To use the servo functions, we must use PWM to control the pulses. Luckily, CircuitPython provides libraries we can use to control servos. To use servo motors, we will need

- The pulseio library – This will allow us to use PWM to control the servo motor.

- The adafruit_motor library – This library contains the functions we need to control the servo motor. The library also provides some functions for working with brushed DC and stepper motors as well. To use this library, we need to copy it to the lib folder on our microcontroller.

Servo Motor with MCU Schematic

We need to use a logic level converter to connect the microcontroller to the servo as the servo runs on 5 volts, but our microcontroller is a 3.3-volt device. This schematic is shown in Figure 9-15.

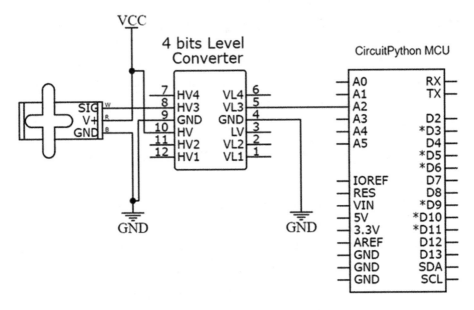

Figure 9-15. *MCU with Servo Schematic*

We connect the circuit as follows:

(1)   Connect the V+ pin of the servo motor to the power rail.

(2)   Connect the GND pin of the servo motor to the GND rail of the breadboard.

(3)   The signal pin is connected to the HV3 pin of the logic level converter.

(4)   Connect LV3 of the logic level converter to pin A2 of the microcontroller.

(5)   Connect the GND pin of the logic level converter to the ground rail on the breadboard.

In Figure 9-16, we see the breadboard version of the circuit.

Figure 9-16. *MCU with Servo Breadboard*

Servo Motor with CircuitPython Program

In order to control the servo motor, we will use the adafruit_motor library functions, and the example will sweep the motor across the 180-degree arc. The program is given in Listing 9-3.

Listing 9-3. Using the Servo Motor Program

```
# import the time library
import time

# import the board pins
import board

# import library for working with PWM
import pulseio

# import library for working with servo
(1) from adafruit_motor import servo

# create a PWMOut object on Pin A2.
(2) pwm = pulseio.PWMOut(board.A2, duty_cycle=2 ** 15,
    frequency=50)
```

```
# Create a servo object, my_servo and set the min and max pulse
(3) my_servo = servo.Servo(pwm, min_pulse = 500, max_pulse = 2800)

(4) while True:
    for angle in range(0, 180, 5):  # 0 - 180 degrees, 5
    degrees at a time.
        my_servo.angle = angle
        time.sleep(0.05)
    for angle in range(180, 0, -5): # 180 - 0 degrees, 5
    degrees at a time.
        my_servo.angle = angle
        time.sleep(0.05)
```

In our program, we perform our usual imports as well as the pulseio library for working with the PWM. At (1) we import the adafruit_motor library to allow us to control the servo motor. At (2) we create a PWM instance on pin A2. At (3) a servo object that we can manipulate is created, and we set the pulse width required to make the servo operate. In the main program loop at (4), we sweep across the range of the servo first from 0 degrees to 180 degrees and then from 180 degrees to 0 degrees.

Feel free to adjust min and max pulse in the my_servo object; the program has been configured to work with the MG90S motor or equivalent.

Stepper Motors

The final motor type we will look at is the stepper motor. Stepper motors are a type of brushless DC motor which of course gives it advantages over the brushed DC motor for some applications. Stepper motors are excellent for positional control which makes them ubiquitous in CNC machines, 3D printers, and plotting machines. Stepper motors also have a high holding torque which makes them uniquely suited for such applications. The disadvantage of stepper motors, however, is that they typically do not run as fast as brushed DC motors due to their construction.

There are two varieties of stepper motors which are bipolar stepper motors and unipolar stepper motors. Regardless of the variety, stepper motors work by energizing coils of wire in phases around a central rotor which have permanent magnet teeth we call poles. The coils of wires are known as stators. These stators are electromagnets that are polarized and depolarized sequentially which allows the motor to rotate in steps. These steps rotate a certain amount of degrees we call the step angle.

The step angle is dependent upon the number of stator poles and rotor teeth within the stepper motor. The stators are energized in phases. These phases of the stators are turned on and off in succession. Doing so creates a magnetic field that causes the rotor to turn, thus creating the stepping action.

A bipolar stepper motor consists of two windings and a motor armature as is shown in Figure 9-17.

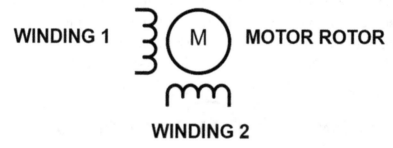

Figure 9-17. *Bipolar Stepper Motor*

The bipolar stepper motor has four wires. You usually refer to your datasheet to determine which two wires belong to which of the winding pairs. The wires are usually color coded for easy identification. If you do not have a datasheet, you can set your multimeter to the continuity range. Using this function, you can check for continuity to determine which pair of wires belong together.

A popular bipolar stepper motor is the 42BYGHM809 which is shown in Figure 9-18.

Figure 9-18. *42BYGHM809 Stepper Motor*

There are also unipolar stepper motors. These motors can come in five-, six-, or eight-pin configurations. Since the six-pin configuration is most common, this is the variety we will be looking at. The schematic diagram for a six-pin unipolar stepper motor is shown in Figure 9-19.

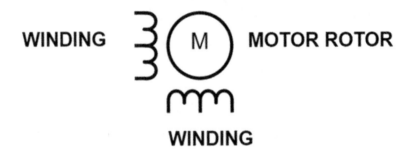

Figure 9-19. *Six-Lead Unipolar Stepper Motor*

Unipolar stepper motors have one winding with a center tap per phase. What this means is that current flows through the coil in only one direction. This can be contrasted with the bipolar stepper motor in which current flows through the coil in both directions.

The six-wire stepper motor we will use is the Sinotech 25BY4801 which represents a generic small stepper motor and is shown in Figure 9-20.

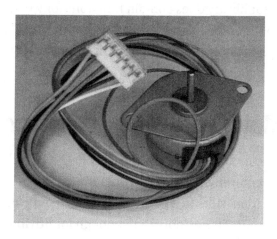

Figure 9-20. *Sinotech 25BY4801 Six-Wire Stepper Motor*

If need be, you can drive the six-lead unipolar stepper motor as a bipolar motor by simply ignoring the center tap.

There are three ways which can be used to drive stepper motors, which are the wave drive mode, the full drive mode, and the half drive mode.

In the wave drive mode, we energize each stator coil on the motor one at a time. What this does is that it gives us less output torque, but it also reduces the power consumed by the motor.

In the full drive mode, we energize two stators at a time, giving us more output torque, which also comes along with more current consumption.

There is also a half drive stepping mode that alternately energizes one, then two phases. It is used to double the angular resolution of the motor (increase the number of steps). Don't worry though; we will only focus on the wave drive and full drive modes which are more intuitive for a beginner to understand.

Stepper Motors in CircuitPython

The adafruit_motor library does contain functions for working with stepper motors both unipolar and bipolar. However, it would be more useful to understand what is going on if we manually drive the motors. For that reason, we will not be using the adafruit_motor library functions.

Stepper Motor with MCU Schematic

For controlling the motor, we will use the ULN2003 IC which can handle the high current requirements of the stepper motor. The ULN2003 contains seven Darlington transistors in a package and can handle up to 500 mA per driver at up to 40v. This is more than enough for driving our motor. The driver also includes suppression diodes which makes it good for driving inductive loads such as our stepper motor. These suppression diodes give added circuit protection. The schematics are given in Figure 9-21.

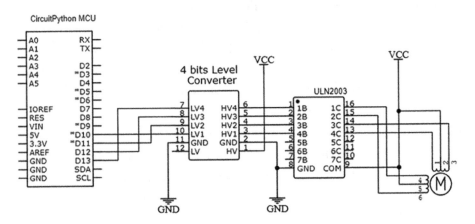

Figure 9-21. *Stepper Motor Control*

We can connect the circuit as follows:

(1) Connect the GND pins of the logic level converter to the ground.

(2) Connect the LV4 pin of the logic level converter to pin D13.

(3) Connect the LV3 pin of the logic level converter to pin D12.

(4) Connect the LV2 pin of the logic level converter to pin D11 and the LV1 pin to pin D10.

(5) On the logic level converter, connect pins HV4, HV3, HV2, and HV1 to pins 1B, 2B, 3B, and 4B of the ULN2003, respectively.

(6) Connect the COM pin of the ULN2003 to pin to VCC.

(7) Connect the center taps 2 and 5 of the stepper motor to VCC.

(8) Connect wires 1 and 3 of the stepper motor to pins 4C and 3C of the ULN2003, respectively.

(9) Connect wires 4 and 6 of the stepper motor to pins 1C and 2C of the ULN2003, respectively.

Since the ULN2003 outputs more current with 5v logic than at 3.3v logic, we use a logic level converter to convert our 3.3-volt signal from the MCU into a 5-volt signal to be used by the ULN2003.

Stepper Motor with CircuitPython Program

We can now write a program to control the stepper motor using the wave drive and full drive modes. The program is given in Listing 9-4. The program is not efficient in terms of compact Python code, but I felt it is easier for a beginner to understand.

Listing 9-4. Using the Stepper Motor Program

```
# import pin constants for board we are using
import board

# import pin control
import digitalio

# import time
import time

(1) # create objects for pins we are using
WHT = digitalio.DigitalInOut(board.D10)
BLK = digitalio.DigitalInOut(board.D11)
YEL = digitalio.DigitalInOut(board.D12)
RED = digitalio.DigitalInOut(board.D13)

(2) # set the pins to output
WHT.direction = digitalio.Direction.OUTPUT
BLK.direction = digitalio.Direction.OUTPUT
YEL.direction = digitalio.Direction.OUTPUT
RED.direction = digitalio.Direction.OUTPUT

(3) # super loop
while True:
    for i in range(24):
        if i < 12:
```

```
# phase 1
# 1000
RED.value = True     # A
BLK.value = False    # B
YEL.value = False    # C
WHT.value = False    # D
time.sleep(0.1)

# phase 2
# 0100
RED.value = False    # A
BLK.value = True     # B
YEL.value = False    # C
WHT.value = False    # D
time.sleep(0.1)

# phase 3
# 0010
RED.value = False    # A
BLK.value = False    # B
YEL.value = True     # C
WHT.value = False    # D
time.sleep(0.1)

# phase 4
0001
RED.value = False    # A
BLK.value = False    # B
YEL.value = False    # C
WHT.value = True     # D
time.sleep(0.1)

time.sleep(0.5)
```

```
else:
    # phase 4
    # 1001
    RED.value = True      # A
    BLK.value = False     # B
    YEL.value = False     # C
    WHT.value = True      # D
    time.sleep(0.1)

    # phase 3
    # 0011
    RED.value = False     # A
    BLK.value = False     # B
    YEL.value = True      # C
    WHT.value = True      # D
    time.sleep(0.1)

    # phase 2
    # 0110
    RED.value = False     # A
    BLK.value = True      # B
    YEL.value = True      # C
    WHT.value = False     # D
    time.sleep(0.1)

    # phase 1
    # 1100
    RED.value = True      # A
    BLK.value = True      # B
    YEL.value = False     # C
    WHT.value = False     # D
    time.sleep(0.1)

    time.sleep(0.5)
```

In our program at (1), we create objects for the pins we are using, and then at (2) we set the pins as output pins. The pins are named according to their wire colors to make the connection easier to follow. At (3) in our main loop, we use the wave drive mode to rotate the motor forward. Then we use the full drive mode to get the motor back to its starting position once we reach 360 degrees of revolution.

In our super loop, when the "i" variable reaches a count of 12, the stepper motor would have completed a full rotation. Since the step angle of the motor is 7.5 degrees and we have four phases in the motor, each time the variable increments, we step four times through 7.5 degrees which is 30 degrees. After 12 counts, we would have rotated 360 degrees.

If you like, you can measure the current draw, and you will see that the full drive mode draws less current than the wave drive mode. In my tests, the full drive mode had a current draw of around 520 milliamps, whereas the wave drive mode had a current draw of around 325 milliamps.

Conclusion

In this chapter, we talked about various DC actuators. We looked at brushed and brushless DC motors, including brushed DC motors, stepper motors, and servo motors. We discussed these characteristics and the use of these motors, as well as how you can interface them with Python-based MCUs. By learning about these topics, we learned about H-Bridges as well as various methods for driving DC motors and wrapped up with programs to control stepper motors. If you need more information, I recommend you look at the manufacturer datasheets for the specific motor drivers including for the L293D and SN754410NE. Robotic arms, mobile robots, and even drone design and control can now be attempted with the knowledge you gained in this chapter.

CHAPTER 10

Python MCU Interfacing

Congratulations! If you made it so far, then you will have covered the basics you need to work with microcontrollers and Python. We have come a long way, but we are not done yet. In this chapter, we will look at using a microcontroller running CircuitPython to interface with some common sensors. The topic of interfacing sensors can cover an entire volume. However, as you go on to building your own projects, there are some sensors you may want to use; in this chapter, we cover sensors you are likely to want to use in your projects.

RGB LED

If you think LEDs are great, then I have a sensor that will knock your socks off. Sometimes, you cannot decide on the color of LED to put in your projects. In such a scenario, we would need to use an LED that contains three LEDs in one package. This is the red, green, and blue or RGB LED. The RGB LED is pictured in Figure 10-1.

© Armstrong Subero 2021
A. Subero, *Programming Microcontrollers with Python*,
https://doi.org/10.1007/978-1-4842-7058-5_10

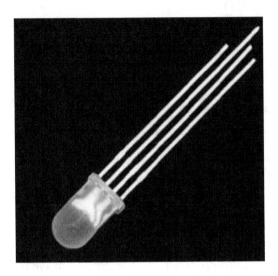

Figure 10-1. *RGB LED Credit: Adafruit, Adafruit.com*

As we learned in our chapter on displays, using the colors red, green, and blue, we will be able to produce any color of light. RGB LEDs have one red, one green, and one blue LED in the same package. Using RGB LEDs, we will be able to produce almost any color of LED we can think of. This makes them great for things like indicators. Instead of having multiple LEDs to relay information, we can have one LED and just vary its color.

The RGB LED has four pins, and the LED may be a common anode or a common cathode. If we look at the RGB LED, we will observe that one pin is longer than the other pins. This long pin can either be connected to the anode or to the cathode of our power supply.

RGB LED with MCU Schematic

We connect the circuit as is shown in Figure 10-2. Our RGB LED is connected to pins D10, D11, and D12. This schematic assumes a common cathode RGB LED is used. If you are using a common anode LED, the longest pin would be connected to VCC instead of the ground.

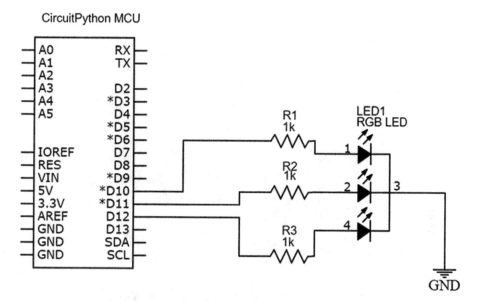

CircuitPython MCU

Figure 10-2. *RGB LED with MCU Schematic*

Note how we use three resistors, since each LED in the package must still be treated like one individual device.

RGB LED Circuit Connection Tips

These are the recommended steps to connect the circuit:

1. Connect the long common pin of your RGB LED to either VCC or the ground depending on which version you have.

2. Connect the remaining three short pins to pins D10, D11, and D12, respectively, using 1k resistors.

When you are finished connecting your circuit, it should look like Figure 10-3.

Figure 10-3. *RGB LED with MCU on Breadboard*

Libraries We'll Need

These are the libraries we will need to add to our lib folder:

- adafruit_rgbled
- simpleio

RGB LED with CircuitPython Program

We can then open our code.py file in the Mu editor so that it resembles Listing 10-1.

Listing 10-1. MCU with RGB LED Program

```
# import board library
import board

# import time library
import time

# import library for RGB led
(1) import adafruit_rgbled

# setup pin constants
(2) RED_LED = board.D10
GREEN_LED = board.D11
BLUE_LED = board.D12

# create a RGB LED object
# invert pwm = false if common cathode
#              true common anode
(3) rgbLed = adafruit_rgbled.RGBLED(RED_LED, GREEN_LED,
    BLUE_LED, invert_pwm=False)

(4) while True:
    # turn on red
    rgbLed.color = (128, 0, 0)
    time.sleep(1)

    # turn on green
    rgbLed.color = (0, 128, 0)
    time.sleep(1)

    # turn on blue
    rgbLed.color = (0, 0, 128)
    time.sleep(1)
```

```
# mix 1
rgbLed.color = (100, 0, 204)
time.sleep(1)

# mix 2
rgbLed.color = (90, 20, 0)
time.sleep(1)
```

We import the modules to set up our board for use. At (1) we import the adafruit_rgbled library which will allow us to control the LED. After we have done this, at (2) then we set up constants for our pin that represents each LED. After this is done, we create an RGB LED object at (3). In our main loop at (4), this object is used where we turn on each individual LED one at a time, red, then green, and then blue for one second each. Then we practice mixing color values.

HC-SR04

Sometimes, you need to measure distance for whatever reason. If you are building a microcontroller-based mobile robot, for instance, you will need to be able to control the direction the robot drives. Using a sensor, to measure the distance the robot is from the object we are using, we can create a semi-intelligent robot. There are two ways we can measure distance, which are using light and sound. Using light is difficult since it is subject to interference from ambient light in the environment. There are resilient light sensors like LIDAR-based sensors; however, these are expensive to integrate into projects. A nice low-cost solution is to use sound. The most used sound sensor is the HC-SR04 sensor which uses ultrasound to measure distance. This sensor is seen in Figure 10-4.

Figure 10-4. *HC-SR04 Ultrasonic SensorCredit: Adafruit, adafruit.com*

The sensor has four pins which are the VCC, GND, a trigger pin, and an echo pin. The device has two ultrasonic transducers. One of the transducers transmits an ultrasonic pulse, and the other device listens for the transmitted pulses. The sensor can measure a distance from 2 cm to 400 cm.

How the sensor works is that the trigger pin (Trig) is used to transmit a pulse from one of the transducers. The echo pin then becomes high when the reflected signal is received. According to the length of the time the device takes to detect a signal on the receive (echo) pin, we can determine the distance of the object we are measuring.

HC-SR04 with MCU Schematic

The circuit connection is given in Figure 10-5. Since the HC-SR04 is a 5-volt device, we need to use a logic level converter to interface it with our CircuitPython MCU. The trigger pin is connected to the MCU via the logic level converter to pin D5, and the echo pin is connected to the MCU via the logic level converter to pin D6.

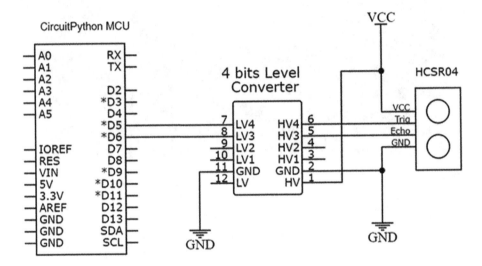

Figure 10-5. *Temperature Sensor with MCU Schematic*

HC-SR04 Circuit Connection Tips

These are the recommended steps to connect the circuit:

1. Connect the VCC pin of your HC-SR04 sensor to the positive rail.

2. Connect the ground pin of the sensor to the ground.

3. Connect the Trig pin of the HC-SR04 to HV4 and the echo pin to HV3.

4. Connect the LV4 pin of the logic level converter to pin D5 and the LV3 pin to pin D6 of the microcontroller.

5. Connect the GND pin of the logic level converter to the negative rail of the breadboard.

When you are finished connecting your circuit, it should look like Figure 10-6.

Figure 10-6. *HC-SR04 with MCU on Breadboard*

Libraries We'll Need

These are the libraries we will need to add to our lib folder:

- adafruit_hcsr04.mpy

HC-SR04 with CircuitPython Program

Edit your code.py in the Mu editor so that it resembles Listing 10-2. This
example is modified from the example provided by Adafruit Industries for
reading the sensor.

Listing 10-2. MCU with Temperature Sensor Program

```
# import time library
import time

# import board library
import board

# import HCSR04 sensor
(1) import adafruit_hcsr04

# create instance of our HCSR04 object
(2) sonar = adafruit_hcsr04.HCSR04(trigger_pin=board.D5,
    echo_pin=board.D6)

# super loop
(3) while True:
    # try to get the distance
    try:
        print((sonar.distance,))

    # else tell us it failed
    except RuntimeError:
        print("Fail!")

    # wait 0.1s
    time.sleep(0.1)
```

In the program, we do our usual imports, and at (1) we import the library allowing us to use the HC-SR04 sensor. At (2) we create an instance of the HCSR04 object we can manipulate, on pins D5 and D6. At (3) in the main super loop, we have a try catch statement that we use to try to read the sensor, and if it fails, we tell the user that an error has occurred. We see the output of the serial console in Figure 10-7.

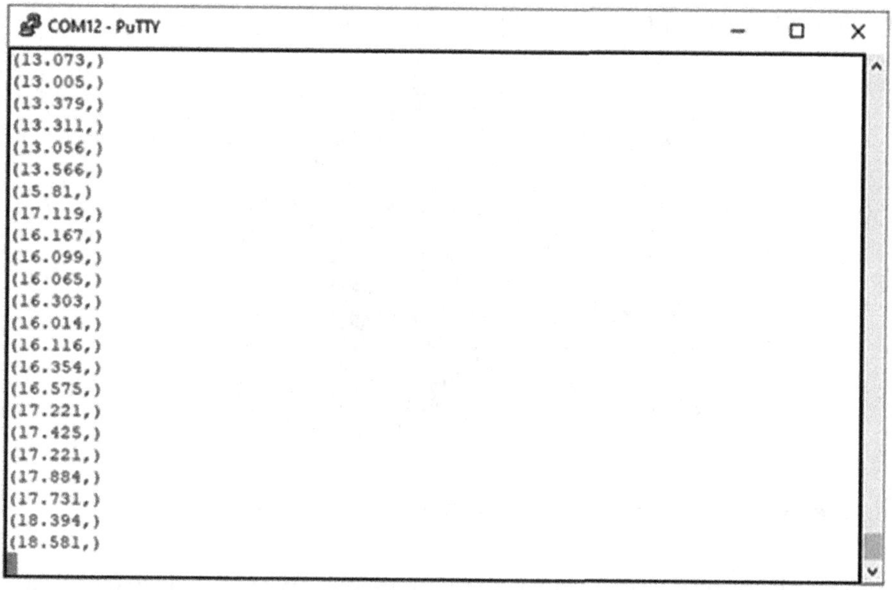

```
COM12 - PuTTY                                    —    □    ×
(13.073,)
(13.005,)
(13.379,)
(13.311,)
(13.056,)
(13.566,)
(15.81,)
(17.119,)
(16.167,)
(16.099,)
(16.065,)
(16.303,)
(16.014,)
(16.116,)
(16.354,)
(16.575,)
(17.221,)
(17.425,)
(17.221,)
(17.884,)
(17.731,)
(18.394,)
(18.581,)
```

Figure 10-7. HC-SR04 Sensor Output

As we move our hand closer to the sensor, the distance reading gets smaller, and as we put our hand away, we observe that the distance reading gets larger.

Piezo Speaker

If you have ever used a microwave or an ATM, you are sure to have heard the electronic beeping that is created from these devices. Sometimes, when we need to alert users of something, we can not only use the light from LEDs, but we can also use sound. The classic way for creating sound is to use a piezoelectric speaker, also called a piezo buzzer or piezo speaker. One such speaker is shown in Figure 10-8.

Figure 10-8. *Piezo Speaker Credit: Adafruit, adafruit.com*

The piezo speaker consists of a tiny metal plate we call a piezo element. The piezo element vibrates when we apply a square wave to it and creates an audible sound. We can use this effect to create a program that allows us to send waves of different frequencies to the device to create different sounds.

Piezo with MCU Schematic

We connect the circuit as is shown in Figure 10-9. The piezo speaker has two pins. We connect the positive pin on the piezo to pin D5 and the other pin to the ground. The positive pin of the piezo usually has a small "+" sign written on the buzzer.

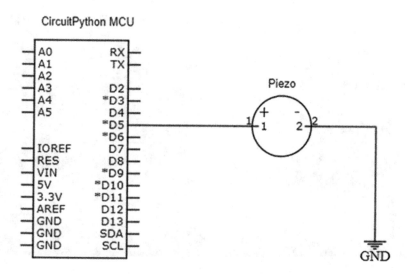

Figure 10-9. *Temperature Sensor with MCU Schematic*

Piezo Circuit Connection Tips

These are the recommended steps to connect the circuit:

1. Connect the ground pin of the piezo speaker to the ground.

2. Connect the positive pin of the piezo to pin D5.

When you are finished connecting your circuit, it should look like Figure 10-10.

Figure 10-10. *Piezo with MCU on Breadboard*

Libraries We'll Need

These are the libraries we will need to add to our lib folder:

- simpleio

Piezo with CircuitPython Program

Edit your code.py in the Mu editor so that it resembles Listing 10-3. This example is modified from the example provided by Adafruit Industries for creating sound.

Listing 10-3. MCU with Piezo Program

```
# import board
import board

# import simple io library
import simpleio
```

```
# Define pin connected to piezo buzzer.
(1) PIEZO_PIN = board.D5

# Define a list of tones/music notes to play.
(2) TONE_FREQ = [ 262,  # C4
                 294,   # D4
                 330,   # E4
                 349,   # F4
                 392,   # G4
                 440,   # A4
                 494 ] # B4

# super loop
(3) while True:
    # Play tones going from start to end of list.
    for i in range(len(TONE_FREQ)):
        simpleio.tone(PIEZO_PIN, TONE_FREQ[i], duration=0.5)

    # Then play tones going from end to start of list.
    for i in range(len(TONE_FREQ)-1, -1, -1):
        simpleio.tone(PIEZO_PIN, TONE_FREQ[i], duration=0.5)
```

In the program, we do our usual imports; then at (1) we set up the piezo to pin D5. At (2) we define a list of notes to play. Using the list of notes in the program, in the super loop at (3), we iterate over them. Once the program works correctly, you will hear the notes coming from your speaker.

DHT11

In the section where we looked at analog interfacing, we looked at using a temperature sensor. However, there is a popular 2-in-1 sensor that can measure temperature and humidity, which is the DHT11 sensor. The DHT11 is pictured in Figure 10-11.

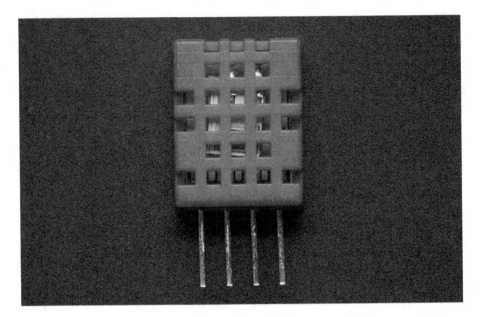

Figure 10-11. *DHT11 Temperature and Humidity Sensor Credit: Adafruit, adafruit.com*

This device has four pins. One pin is VCC, and the other pin is the ground pin. There is also an output pin that we use to read the data from the sensor.

DHT11 with MCU Schematic

We connect the circuit as is shown in Figure 10-12. We connect the output of the DHT11 to our input pin D10. To operate properly, we need a pull-up resistor connected to the output pin of the DHT11.

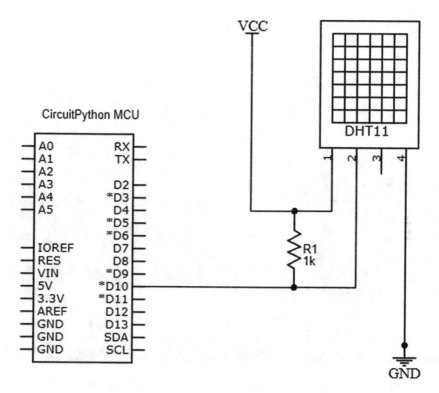

Figure 10-12. *DHT11 Sensor with MCU Schematic*

DHT11 Sensor Circuit Connection Tips

These are the recommended steps to connect the circuit:

1. Connect the VCC pin of your DHT11 to the positive rail.

2. Connect the ground pin of the sensor to the ground.

3. Connect the 1k resistor from the output pin to the VCC pin.

4. Run a jumper wire from the output pin of the DHT11 sensor to pin D10 on the MCU running CircuitPython.

When you are finished connecting your circuit, it should look like Figure 10-13.

Figure 10-13. *Temperature Sensor with MCU on Breadboard*

Libraries We'll Need

These are the libraries we will need to add to our lib folder:

- adafruit_dht

DHT11 Sensor with CircuitPython Program

Edit your code.py in the Mu editor so that it resembles Listing 10-4. This example is modified from the example provided by Adafruit Industries for reading the sensor.

Listing 10-4. MCU with DHT11 Sensor Program

```
# import board
import board

# import time
import time

# import busio
import busio

# import library for working with sensor
(1) import adafruit_dht

# connect the DHT11 to pin10
(2) dht = adafruit_dht.DHT11(board.D10)

(3) while True:
    try:
        # read the temperature and humidity
        temperature = dht.temperature
        humidity = dht.humidity

        # print the read temepratue and humidity
        print("Temp: {:.1f} *C \t Humidity: {}%".
        format(temperature, humidity))

    except RuntimeError as e:
        # if dosent work print error
        print("Reading from DHT failure: ", e.args)

    # print every second
    time.sleep(1)
```

In the program, we do our usual imports; then at (1) we import the library for working with the DHT11 sensor. At (2) we create an instance of the DHT11 sensor on pin 10. In our main loop at (3), we read the temperature and humidity of the sensor and print it to the console. The output is shown in Figure 10-14.

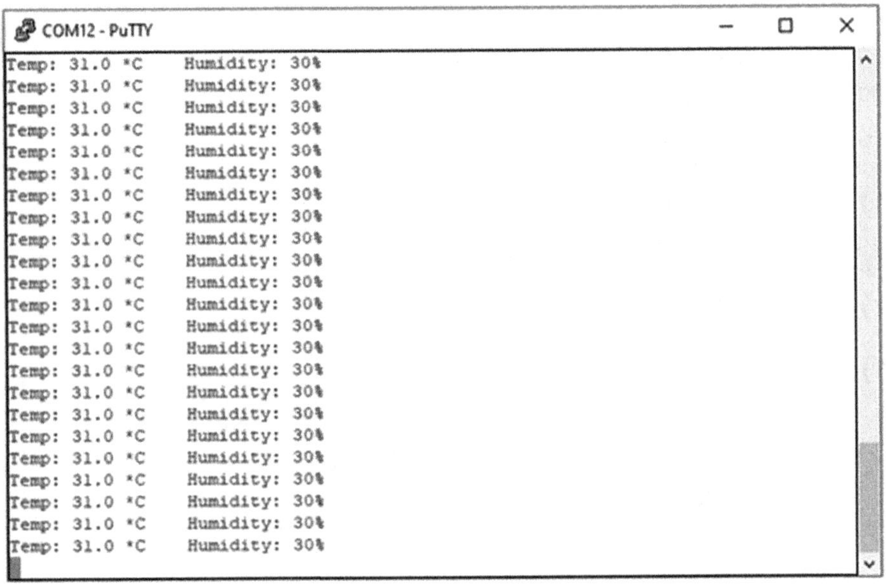

Figure 10-14. *DHT11 Sensor Output*

The sensor will output data at a steady rate, and thanks to our try catch, if the program fails, it will keep running and output data to the console.

Note that even though this example uses the DHT11 sensor, the DHT22 can also be used without any problems as the "adafruit_dht" library supports both devices. To use this sensor when creating an instance of the sensor, you would simply change DHT11 to DHT22.

Conclusion

In this chapter, we looked at interfacing some common sensors using MicroPython-based microcontrollers. We looked at using RGB LEDs, ultrasonic sensors, sound, and temperature and humidity sensors. The knowledge gained in this chapter will allow you to build some remarkably interesting embedded systems.

Congratulations! You have worked through the entire book. If you made it this far, then you would have built a solid foundation for using CircuitPython with microcontrollers. Don't stop there! There is still a lot you can do to increase your knowledge. Examine the Adafruit libraries bundle and run the code samples from there. Keep tinkering!

Index

© Armstrong Subero 2021
A. Subero, *Programming Microcontrollers with Python,*
https://doi.org/10.1007/978-1-4842-7058-5

Printed in the United States
by Baker & Taylor Publisher Services